OLDEST HOUSTON

LYDIA SCHRANDT
& BIJU SUKUMARAN

REEDY PRESS

Copyright © 2022
All rights reserved.
Reedy Press
PO Box 5131
St. Louis, MO 63139
www.reedypress.com

No part of this publication may be reproduced or transmitted in any form or by any means, electronic or mechanical, including photocopy, recording, or any information storage and retrieval system, without permission in writing from the publisher. Permissions may be sought directly from Reedy Press at the above mailing address or via our website at www.reedypress.com.

We (the publisher and the author) have done our best to provide the most accurate information available when this book was completed. However, we make no warranty, guarantee, or promise about the accuracy, completeness, or currency of the information provided, and we expressly disclaim all warranties, expressed or implied. Please note that attractions, company names, addresses, websites, and phone numbers are subject to change or closure, and this is outside of our control. We are not responsible for any loss, damage, injury, or inconvenience that may occur due to the use of this book.

Library of Congress Control Number: 2021950833

ISBN: 9781681063621

Cover Design: Jill Halpin
Book Design: Linda Eckels

Interior photos by the authors unless otherwise noted.

Cover photo credit, clockwise from top left: 400 Block of Main Street (University of Houston Libraries Digital Collections), Kellum-Noble House (Library of Congress), Annunciation Church (Wikimedia Commons), Downtown scene (Houston Public Library Digital Archives).

Printed in the United States of America
22 23 24 25 26   5 4 3 2 1

Dedication

To Biju's parents, Valsala and Anakara Sukumaran, for taking a chance on this city of jumbled cultures so long ago.

To Lydia's parents, Judi and Bill Schrandt, for instilling a love of reading, learning, and adventuring.

To Justin Seth James, for always inspiring us to explore places near and far.

And to James Byron Adams, for continually demonstrating how great Houston truly is (especially when compared to Dallas).

Table of Contents

Acknowledgments viii
Introduction ix

Downtown

Oldest Tree 2
Oldest Port 4
Oldest Religious Congregation 6
Oldest Building 8
Oldest Commercial Building 10
Oldest Law Firm 12
Oldest Catholic Church 14
Oldest Catholic School 16
Oldest Hospital 18
Oldest Performing Arts Organization 19
Oldest Hotel 21
Oldest Skyscraper 23
Oldest Theater Company 25
Oldest Permanent Opera Company 27
Oldest Chinese Restaurant 28
Oldest Martin Luther King Day Parade in the
    United States 30
Oldest Art Car Parade in the World 32

West Inner Loop

Oldest Cemetery 35
Oldest Black Neighborhood 37
Oldest Professionally Designed Cemetery 39

Oldest African American Cemetery 41
Oldest Intact Neighborhood 43
Oldest Boot Maker 45
Oldest Suburb 47
Oldest Firehouse 49
Oldest Brick-Paved Street 50
Oldest University 52
Oldest Local Fast-Food Chain 54
Oldest Outdoor Theater 56
Oldest Museum 58
Oldest Statue 60
Oldest Underground Reservoir 62
Oldest Public Garden 64
Oldest Ice House 66
Oldest Fish Market 68
Oldest Bakery 69
Oldest BBQ Joint 70
Oldest Hardware Store 72
Oldest Doughnut Shop 73
Oldest Cafeteria 74
Oldest Fountain 76
Oldest Bar 77
Oldest Deli 78
Oldest Gay Organization 79
Oldest Tobacconist 81
Oldest Stadium 82
Oldest Sports Bar 84
Oldest Italian Restaurant 85
Oldest Hindu Temple 87
Oldest Bookstore 89

TABLE OF CONTENTS **V**

Oldest Comic Shop 91
Oldest Crawfish Restaurant... 93
Oldest Vietnamese Restaurant... 95

East Inner Loop
Oldest African American Church 98
Oldest Park... 100
Oldest 18-Hole Golf Course 102
Oldest Recording Studio... 104
Oldest Soul Food Restaurant 106
Oldest Fajita Restaurant.. 108
Oldest Craft Brewery 110

West and Southwest
Oldest Jewish Congregation in Texas 113
Oldest Haberdashery 115
Oldest Women's Club... 117
Oldest Independent, Nonparochial School............................. 119
Oldest Country Club... 121
Oldest Restaurant 123
Oldest Burger Joint... 125
Oldest Tex-Mex Restaurant... 127
Oldest Pizza Parlor.. 129
Oldest Indian Restaurant.. 130

South Side and Southeast
Oldest Commercial Airport... 133
Oldest Urban Expressway... 135

Oldest Muslim Community 137
Oldest Continuously Operating Opera Company 139
Oldest Public Television Station 141
Oldest Kolache Shop 143
Oldest Buddhist Temple 145

TREASURES OUTSIDE THE CITY
Oldest Operating Ferry 148
Oldest Town in Harris County 149
Oldest Newspaper in Texas 151
Oldest Business in Texas 153
Oldest Funeral Home in Texas 155
Oldest Drugstore in Texas 157
Oldest Oil Field 159
Oldest Library in Texas 161
Oldest Hatter 163
Oldest Seafood Restaurant in Texas 165
Oldest Barber Shop in Texas 167
Oldest Tex-Mex Restaurant in Texas 169
Oldest Butcher 170

Sources 172
Index 181

ACKNOWLEDGMENTS

Today we call it Houston, Bayou City, the Energy Capital of the World. The history presented in this book largely begins in 1836, but long before that, Native American peoples were connected to this land. We would like to acknowledge that the city we call home occupies the ancestral lands of the Karankawa, Coahuiltecan, Atakapa Ishak, and Sana. Indigenous people from these and other Native American nations live and work in this region today. To learn more about land acknowledgment, please visit usdac.us/nativeland.

Through researching and writing this book, we've drawn on numerous resources. The Texas State Historical Association's *Handbook of Texas* and the University of North Texas's Portal to Texas History proved invaluable for tracking down primary source materials and interesting tidbits. The brilliant work presented in the pages of *Houston History* magazine, published by the Center for Public History at the University of Houston, inspired us to dig deeper to find the story behind the story.

Several individuals took time out of their days to assist us, including Teresa Brewer (and the board) of the Black Heritage Society, Howard Huffstutler with the Diana Foundation, Zion Escobar with the Houston Freedmen's Town Conservancy, Lynn Cooper Hinrichs with the Gilbert and Sullivan Society of Houston, Brian Mitchell with the Houston Grand Opera, John Rovell with the Kinkaid School, Abbie Falk with the Houston Fire Museum, Jessica McFall with the Buffalo Bayou Partnership, and the staff at the Houston Metropolitan Research Center.

Introduction

To many visitors and residents, Houston is a never-ending tableau of highways and construction.

There was a time in the not-so-distant past where Space City was obsessed only with the future. The steady growth of concrete, from strip malls to overpasses, was fed by the inexorable annexation of suburbs. Urban sprawl, like a rapidly expanding forest, has overgrown old neighborhoods, buildings, and even towns.

When driving hours to far-flung parts of the city, it's easy to overlook gems of bygone eras. But it was here that pioneers eked out a living on the banks of bayous; in the late 1800s and early 1900s, it's where wildcatters made their fortunes and immigrants dared to dream big. At the edges of the map, the impossible somehow seemed a bit more probable.

In many ways, Houston still is the Wild West.

With the city's incredibly liberal zoning laws, you're likely to find a hidden bar, or even a Buddhist monastery, tucked away without fanfare amidst innocuous residential neighborhoods—if you're willing to stray off course and sneak a look around the corner.

Throughout its history, Houston has always been a city of juxtaposition. And with so many recent waves of immigration adding new layers and patina to the old, it's even more so today.

According to the past two censuses, Houston is one of the most diverse cities in the US. In 2016, *Black Enterprise* magazine called Houston "the next great Black business Mecca." Houston has been home to not one, not two, but three Asian towns, and that's not including "Little India" (now the Mahatma Gandhi District), the South Asian enclaves to the south, or even "Little Cambodia" just outside the city.

There's a reason why jet-set luminaries like Anthony Bourdain and David Chang were so intrigued by the city's food scene—you can truly find the world here.

But what's perhaps most curious is how blasé it all is. Houstonians are as utterly unfazed by a Pakistani Tex-Mex food truck as they are by a Hindu temple next door.

The pandemic put a damper on the city as events, festivals, communities, and historic businesses that withstood the test of time shuttered. But Houston has dealt with other calamities before—hurricanes, fires, booms, and busts. It's been an improbable town from the very start. City founders Augustus Chapman and John Kirby Allen sold Houston, situated on a swamp, as a "beautifully elevated" city depicted among towering hills with a fresh sea breeze.

With the heroic efforts of a number of historic and preservation societies, that complex history is being brought to light. In this book, we've attempted to showcase this melting pot of not only culture but also intergenerational stories—the people, the places, and their struggles and times. We've tried to highlight many of the often-underrepresented groups to show the good and the bad.

Houston still houses the Energy Corridor and still boasts some of the most cutting-edge medical research in the world. The National Aeronautics and Space Administration (NASA) still plans on strapping cowboys onto rockets. But the hope is that this book will inspire you to step into the past, pause by that historic marker, support that old business, and explore one street back.

DOWNTOWN

---1600

OLDEST TREE
Old Hanging Oak
666-698 Bagby St.

Local legend has it that Houston's oldest tree once served as a makeshift gallows during the Republic of Texas era (1836-1845), when as many as 11 men were hanged from its branches. Historians have since concluded that no one actually was ever hanged from the tree—its shade instead served as a shelter for mourners and onlookers. But other trees in the neighborhood likely did serve this sinister purpose.

In fact, many towns in the American West during the frontier days had a "hanging tree"—often near the courthouse—where public executions were carried out. You can find such trees, surrounded by an amalgam of historical fact and macabre fiction, in the small Texas towns of Bandera, Brazoria, Goliad, and Coldspring.

The legend of Houston's Old Hanging Oak could very well date to Wednesday, March 28, 1838. Convicted murderers John Christopher Columbus Quick and David James Jones were hanged at a gallows described by a newspaper article at the time as being "in a beautiful islet of timber, situated in the prairie about a mile south of the city." The area soon became known as Hangman's Grove, but its exact location in Houston is contested among modern historians.

The Old Hanging Oak, believed to be some 400 years old, stands at the corner of Bagby and Capitol Streets in downtown

Houston. Its purported sordid history aside, this particular Texas live oak (*Quercus fusiformis*) was there at the birth of Houston as a city, when the Allen brothers first stepped foot on the banks of Buffalo Bayou in 1837. And it should stick around well into the future; the oldest live oaks in the nation are several hundred to more than 1,000 years old.

Find the Old Hanging Oak in the heart of the Houston Theater District near Little Tranquility Park, two blocks northeast of City Hall. Walk three blocks southwest along Bagby Street to visit Sam Houston Park and its collection of historic 19th-century houses.

DOWNTOWN 3

1836

OLDEST PORT
ALLEN'S LANDING
1005 Commerce St.

Allen's Landing. The birthplace of Houston. Houston's Plymouth Rock. The place where it all started. At least that's how the story goes. It was here at the confluence of Buffalo and White Oak Bayous that August Chapman and John Kirby Allen, two entrepreneurial brothers from New York, claimed Houston as their own.

The pair had purchased 8,850 acres of prairie swamp and named it after the hero of the Battle of San Jacinto, General Sam Houston.

August 30, 1836, the day celebrated as Houston's birthday, was not in fact the day the Allen brothers first came ashore on the banks of the bayou, nor was it the day they purchased the land. Instead, Houston's founding day was the day the Allen brothers took out an advertisement in the *Telegraph* and *Texas Register*, the official newspaper of the Republic of Texas.

"There is no place in Texas more healthy," the brothers wrote, "having an abundance of excellent spring water, and enjoying the sea breeze in all its freshness."

Any modern Houstonian would likely laugh out loud at that bald-faced lie, but the sales pitch worked. Houston's population began to grow. The Allen brothers weren't wrong about everything. They rightly predicted (or at least wished for) Houston's status as a critical trade center.

"Allen's Landing" (1910). Photo courtesy of the Museum of Houston and the Houston Metropolitan Research Center

"The town of Houston is located at a point on the river which must ever command the trade of the largest and richest portion of Texas," they wrote in the same ad. "When the rich lands of the country shall be settled, a trade will flow to it, making it, beyond all doubt, the great interior commercial emporium of Texas."

Soon after the founding of Houston, the area now known as Allen's Landing became Houston's first port, a natural turning basin for vessels. A wooden dock served cargo ships carrying cotton, rice, sugar, and coffee up and down the bayou for nearly a century.

In 1914, the turning basin for ships relocated to the newly dredged Houston Ship Channel, and the port at the base of Main Street fell out of use. Today, a 1.76-acre park memorializes the spot's history with a reconstruction of the historic port.

Allen's Landing is on the south bank of Buffalo Bayou, just a couple blocks from historic Market Square Park. The Old Spaghetti Warehouse, adjacent to Allen's Landing, is rumored to be among the most haunted buildings in downtown.

―――――――――――――――――1839

Oldest Religious Congregation
Christ Church Cathedral
1117 Texas Ave.

There were Protestant Episcopals in Mexican Texas, but these small communities could not practice their faith openly under the law of the Catholic church. When the Christ Church Cathedral congregation was established on March 16, 1839, it was one of the first non-Roman Catholic churches in the state and the first religious congregation in Houston. It's also the only congregation still worshipping on its original site from when Texas was a republc.

Col. William Fairfax Gray founded the congregation with 28 cosigners of a paper declaring the mission to "unite together as a Christian congregation in the city of Houston—to observe the forms of worship and be governed by the Constitution of the Protestant Episcopal Church in the United States of North America." With support from 45 Houstonians, including the city's founder, Augustus Allen, the congregation purchased the half block it still occupies for $400.

The congregation quickly outgrew its original 1845 church building and laid the cornerstone for a new structure in 1859. A cattleman passing with his herd en route to Kansas City donated one of his steers to the church; the steer's head on the Diocesan Seal is a nod to his generosity.

The Civil War slowed construction, and the first service wasn't held in the new building until Easter of 1876. That structure would collapse during an 1893 expansion, and yet another new structure was built in a Gothic Revival style. This one, the current church building, held its first service on Christmas Eve in 1893.

Christ Church Cathedral now operates as a cathedral church—a seat of an Episcopal bishop (in this case, the bishop of the Episcopal Diocese of Texas). Many other Episcopal churches in the area got their starts as missions of Christ Church.

Daily services in English and Spanish are open to everyone. Visit on Sunday evening to attend a Celtic-inspired worship service featuring muted lighting, Celtic music played on the harp and cello, and prayers from communities in Ireland and Scotland.

Christ Church Cathedral is in downtown Houston, just a few blocks from historic Market Square Park and across the street from The Sam, Houston's oldest hotel.

―――――――――――――――1847

Oldest Building
Kellum-Noble House
212 Dallas St.

The Kellum-Noble House, the oldest surviving building still standing on its original foundations, was built in 1847 by Nathaniel Kellum. Kellum arrived in a young Houston in 1839 during the Republic of Texas. He built his L-shaped home—arguably the grandest in Houston at the time—with bricks from his own brickyard and clay from Buffalo Bayou. Kellum was a slave owner, and it was likely enslaved men who molded and kiln-fired the bricks that make up the home's walls.

When the Kellum family relocated to Grimes County in 1848, Abram and Zerviah Noble purchased the home. Abram Noble put up several of his slaves as collateral for the loan he used to purchase the house. Their names and ages, recorded on the paperwork, were Frank (36), Willis (26), "Doc" or Ambrose (28), Mary (22), Sam (3), Jake (2 months), and Harriet (14).

By the 1870s, Zerviah had opened a school in her home; in 1872, there were 36 students enrolled. For a brief time, it operated as a public school—among the first in Houston. During the extensive restoration work that began in 2014, archaeologists found pencil lead and slate in the dirt that had been removed from beneath the floorboards.

After the city purchased the estate in 1899 as part of its first municipal park, the house and grounds served several functions. It was the park keeper's residence, parks department headquarters, and briefly the first zoo in Houston, home to a pair of wolves named King and Queen (among other animals).

In 1954, a freeway project put the home at risk for demolition. The Heritage Society was founded to protect and restore the site. Today, the Heritage Society offers docent-led tours of the historic house museum, furnished to depict life in the mid-19th century.

The Kellum-Noble House occupies the southwest portion of Sam Houston Park in downtown. The park is home to nine other historical buildings, each relocated to the park and restored by the Heritage Society. Houston City Hall sits catty-corner from the park to the northeast, and just beyond that, you'll find the Theater District. The park sits along Buffalo Bayou Park, not far from the Buffalo Bayou Park Cistern.

Photo courtesy of Historic American Buildings Survey (Library of Congress)

1860

Oldest Commercial Building
Kennedy Bakery
813 Congress St.

During the late 19th century, Market Square Park served as Houston's first commercial district. The narrow, red brick building at 813 Congress Street ranks as the oldest commercial building still standing.

The structure was built around 1860 after a fire destroyed the previous 1847 wooden building. The Kennedy Building gets its name from its first owner, Irish immigrant John Kennedy, who commissioned the building as a new home for his steam bakery.

According to local lore, he obtained a contract during the Civil War to bake hardtack for the Confederate Army.

Kennedy would go on to become one of Houston's wealthiest businessmen, owning all the buildings on that side of the block—an area known as Kennedy's Corner. He passed away in 1878.

The Kennedy Bakery building remained in the Kennedy family until 1970. Over its more than a century of existence, it housed a trading post, stagecoach stop, drugstore, and coffee shop. Most recently, the historic structure has been home to one of Houston's oldest watering holes, La Carafe.

This beloved local wine bar opened in the mid-1950s, and the interior hasn't changed much since. A *Houston Press* writer during the 1960s described the space as having "nuances of New Orleans, glimmerings of Greenwich Village, and leanings toward the Left Bank of Paris." Patrons sip wine and Texas craft brews at the candlelit bar and pay their tabs—cash only—on a hand-cranked, 1914, brass National cash register. A classic jukebox plays tunes from decades past.

While La Carafe may not be Houston's oldest bar—that designation goes to Leon's Lounge—it is believed to be one of the most haunted. Reported spectral sightings include that of a former bar manager named Carl spotted through the windows at night, a woman in white wandering the second floor, and a young boy bouncing a ball.

The Kennedy Bakery building sits on the northeast side of Market Square Park in downtown Houston. The green space includes a dog run, performance space, and public art installations, and several other restaurants and bars border the park. Notable among them is Warren's Inn, another classic bar under the same ownership as La Carafe.

DOWNTOWN **11**

———————————————1866
OLDEST LAW FIRM
BAKER BOTTS LLP
910 Louisiana St.

B aker Botts, an international law firm with 725 practicing lawyers and offices in London, Hong Kong, Riyadh, and Brussels, got its start in Houston circa 1866.

Texas legislature member and Confederate Army Lieutenant Colonel Walter Browne Botts, and Army of the Republic of Texas Captain Peter W. Gray, founded Gray and Botts to practice trial and railroad law.

District judge James Addison Baker Sr. and his son James Addison Baker Jr., personal lawyer of William Marsh Rice, joined the firm in the 1870s, around the time when Gray died. The firm became Baker, Botts, and Baker. The younger Baker played a key role in the litigation which proved that Rice was murdered and revalidated his will that endowed Rice University.

That wouldn't be the end of the Baker legacy at the firm. James A. Baker III, former White House chief of staff and secretary of the treasury for President Ronald Reagan, and secretary of state and White House chief of staff for George H. W. Bush, joined the firm after leaving public service in 1993. The firm had to rewrite its no-nepotism rule to allow Baker III to practice.

George W. Bush once worked in the mailroom when he was 15 years old.

Today, Baker Botts ranks among the world's foremost law firms representing the energy sector, with a client list that includes Exxon Mobil, Shell Oil, and Halliburton. In 1874, the firm generated $26,000 in revenue. In 2020, that number hit $710.8 million.

Some of the firm's client relationships go back more than a century. One such client, CenterPoint Energy, hired the firm in 1882 when CenterPoint was called Houston Light & Power. Baker Botts has handled much of the power company's legal work ever since.

Peter W. Gray, one of the founders of Baker Botts, also was a founder of Houston Lyceum, which would go on to become the Houston Public Library. The Julia Ideson Building, a Houston Public Library facility, sits catty-corner to One Shell Plaza, the downtown Houston home of Baker Botts.

1871
OLDEST CATHOLIC CHURCH
CHURCH OF THE ANNUNCIATION
1618 Texas Ave.

In the years after the Civil War, money was tight, and the congregation of St. Vincent's–Houston's first Catholic church– quickly was outgrowing the old building. Father Joseph Querat, a missionary to Texas from France, and Claude M. Dubuis, the bishop of Galveston, came together to build a new church for the community.

Building materials were scarce at the time. Bishop Dubuis purchased a half-block of land for $2,000 and an old courthouse for $1,000. He used the cleaned and dismantled bricks to build the church's foundation. Local Houstonians raised the remaining funds through a series of local community events.

Father Querat designed the structure after the Gothic cathedrals of Europe. The cornerstone was placed in 1869, and the church was dedicated on September 10, 1871. The Gothic bell tower, designed by Texas architect Nicholas J. Clayton, was added later, making the church the tallest structure in Houston at the time. Clayton, known for his church architecture, also completely redesigned the interior, thickened the nave walls, and added a clerestory level.

Other additions over the years included a replica of Raphael's *The Transfiguration* inside the church dome, a rose window, a Pilcher pipe organ, and a pair of marble shrines to Our Lady of Perpetual Help and Our Lady, Help of Christians.

The Church of Annunciation has played a foundational role in expanding the Catholic community in Houston. Since its founding, five offspring parishes have formed from the mother parish: St. Joseph, St. Patrick, St. Nicholas, Sacred Heart, and Blessed Sacrament.

Annunciation sits just across Texas Street from Minute Maid Park, home of the Houston Astros. You can buy Astros-themed rosaries at the church entrance during weekend home games. Three blocks southwest, at the corner of Crawford and McKinney Streets, is Discovery Green, a downtown park with a lake, playground, dog run, restaurants, and a winter skating rink. If you continue down Texas Street past US 59, you'll find BBVA Stadium, where the Houston Dynamo FC and Houston Dash play.

1873
OLDEST CATHOLIC SCHOOL
INCARNATE WORD ACADEMY
609 Crawford St.

You wouldn't know by looking at the modern façade that Incarnate Word Academy, on the corner of Jackson and Crawford in downtown Houston, holds the distinction of being the city's oldest Catholic school.

A lot has changed since the first Mass was held on May 5, 1873—a day celebrated by faculty and students as Foundation Day. During the school's early years, the daughters of Houston's oldest families enrolled in Incarnate Word as a finishing school, where they took classes in things like home economics and china painting. It wasn't until the early 20th century that the focus shifted to college prep.

Today, the 300-odd young women who attend the Catholic high school are equipped with personal iPads and study in classrooms outfitted with smartboard technology. And the student body reflects the diversity of the city it calls home.

The school's story began in 1872, when Mother Mary Gabriel Dillion and two other Sisters of the Incarnate Word and Blessed Sacrament traveled to Texas from Lyon, France. Father John Odin, the bishop of Galveston, summoned the sisters to establish a school for young women.

The sisters arrived in Houston on April 25, 1873, and took up residence in a former Franciscan monastery downtown. Less than two weeks later, school was in session.

Incarnate Word debuted a grand, Romanesque-style convent in 1905. Irish American architect Nicholas Clayton designed the building—one of his few works in Houston. Despite protests and opposition from former students, the historic red brick building was razed in 2015 to make way for a more modern academic building. You can still see Clayton's work at the Church of the Annunciation next door, where he designed the Gothic bell tower.

Incarnate Word has resisted encouragement to relocate and has chosen to continue serving the downtown Houston community. Students have the fourth-largest city in the US right at their doorstep, including the oldest church (Church of the Annunciation) right next door, and Discovery Green and Minute Maid Park each just a block away.

―――――――――――――――1887

Oldest Hospital
St. Joseph Medical Center
1401 St. Joseph Pkwy.

Photo courtesy of the Museum of Houston and the Houston Metropolitan Research Center

Medicine is a big industry in Houston. The 61-institution Texas Medical Center ranks as the largest in the world, home to the world's largest children's hospital and the world's largest cancer hospital.

While the Texas Medical Center got its start in the early 20th century, Houston's hospital history dates back even further, to June 1, 1887.

It was on this day that the Sisters of Charity of the Incarnate Word opened a small infirmary and what would become the city's first hospital. St. Joseph Medical Center in downtown met a clear need for Houstonians and expanded many times over the decades. The staff served the city through the Spanish flu, the Texas City disaster, Hurricane Harvey, and the COVID-19 pandemic.

It was a hospital of firsts—the first emergency care facility, the first teaching hospital, and the first obstetrics department in Houston. At one time, it was nicknamed "Houston's birthplace," as 9 of 10 native Houstonians were born here.

If you're curious to learn more about the history of medicine in Houston, visit the Wallace D. Wilson Museum at the Texas Heart Institute, the Health Museum, or the DeBakey Library and Museum, which features a recreated operating room.

1913
Oldest Performing Arts Organization
Houston Symphony
615 Louisiana St.

Among the first-known performances of orchestral music in Houston was a small ensemble who performed at the Exchange Saloon. Performances by visiting orchestras throughout the opening decade of the 20th century whet Houston's appetite for a permanent orchestra of its own.

Philanthropist and art collector Ima Hogg helped raise the money to found the Houston Symphony. On June 21, 1913, the 35-member orchestra took the stage at the Majestic Theater in downtown Houston, under the musical direction of Belgian-born Julien Paul Blitz. The outing was a success, and aside from being disbanded during World War I, the orchestra has been entertaining Houstonians ever since as one of the oldest performing arts organizations in the nation.

Throughout its more than a century of performances, the Houston Orchestra made its home at several venues around town, including the Palace Theatre, City Auditorium, and the Houston Music Hall. During World War II, the orchestra often would perform at military bases in Texas and Louisiana.

Photo courtesy of the Houston Symphony

On October 2, 1966, the orchestra played for the first time in its new home, the Jones Hall for the Performing Arts. The building won the prestigious American Institute of Architects' Honor Award the next year for its innovative design.

Some 800 hexagons comprise a movable ceiling that can alter the sound quality within the space. Golden teak walls surround the space, where red velvet seats can accommodate an audience of up to 2,300 people.

Despite the multimillion-dollar loss of the music library and numerous instruments due to flooding from Tropical Storm Allison in 2001 and a canceled season during the COVID-19 pandemic, the Houston Symphony has endured. Today, the Grammy-winning ensemble includes 88 professional musicians who perform 170 concerts—a mix of classical, pops, and family programming—annually. They're one of Houston's most active performing arts organizations.

Jones Hall, home of the Houston Symphony, sits at the heart of the downtown Theater District, catty-corner to the Alley Theatre (the oldest theater company in the city).

1924

OLDEST HOTEL
THE SAM HOUSTON
1117 Prairie St.

The post–World War I era brought with it a population boom in Houston. With the growth came a new type of traveler—the business traveler.

The Sam Houston Hotel opened its doors in 1924 as a 200-room property, designed to offer an affordable option for business travelers with an overnight layover at nearby Union Rail Station (now Minute Maid Park). The hotel was named after Sam Houston, the first president of the Republic of Texas and the state's seventh governor. His son, Colonel A. J. Houston, was the first man to register in the hotel guest book.

Compared to the more luxurious hotels downtown at the time, the Sam Houston was decidedly simple. An October 1924 article in the *Houston Post-Dispatch* described the interior: "Everything in the hotel, while modern and most beautiful, will be plain, no attempt having been made to add the many frills which usually feature present-day hotel construction."

An advertisement painted across the party wall outside read, "No rooms over $2.50. No room under $2.00." That extra 50 cents got you a private bathroom.

But that didn't mean the hotel was without its comforts. The hotel also advertised itself as having air-conditioning. Modern air-conditioning wasn't actually installed until 1937, but the hotel did feature transom windows and louvers built into the doors to promote air circulation. The *Houston Post-Dispatch* described it as "one of the best ventilated hotel structures in the state."

Economic hardship in the 1970s led to the shuttering of the hotel in 1975. It remained vacant until 2002, when it reopened after extensive renovations. It also was added to the National Register of Historic Places for its architecture—the hotel is considered an excellent example of early high-rise construction.

> *Today, the Sam Houston Hotel is a 100-room boutique property, part of the CURIO Collection by Hilton. Its location in the heart of downtown on Prairie Street is within walking distance of the George R. Brown Convention Center, Discovery Green, Minute Maid Park (home of the Houston Astros baseball team), and the Theater District.*

————————————1927
OLDEST SKYSCRAPER
NIELS ESPERSON BUILDING
808 Travis St.

The Niels Esperson Building is not only Houston's oldest skyscraper—the tallest building in Texas at the time it was built—it's also among the grandest and most expensive gestures of love.

When oil and real estate tycoon Niels Esperson passed away in 1922, he left his wife, Mellie Keenan Esperson, his substantial wealth and a dream for a building he'd envisioned for one of his downtown properties.

In 1924, Mellie traveled to Europe to get inspiration for the structure—Niels had left no specific plans. Upon her return, she commissioned John Eberson, a prominent Chicago architect known for his work on movie palaces and opera houses, to design a 32-story Italian Renaissance memorial to her husband.

The Niels Esperson Building opened in 1927 as the third-tallest structure in the nation, at 411 feet tall. The price tag was $4 million, or what would be about $58 million today. Mellie's vision included architectural details such as imported Roman marble, terra cotta urns, Corinthian columns, bronze elevator doors, and a *tempietto* (a domed "little temple") atop its gold leaf tower. Air-conditioning was added in 1938, and it remains the only complete example of Italian Renaissance architecture in the downtown area.

Fourteen years later, Mellie commissioned Eberson and his brother Drew to design an adjoining building. The 19-story, Art Deco–style Mellie Esperson Building was completed in 1941. It was notably the first skyscraper in Houston to be built with central air-conditioning.

Mellie joined her husband on January 14, 1945. Some believe her spirit still walks the halls and rides the grand elevators.

Though no longer the tallest, the two Esperson buildings still stand side by side.

The JPMorgan Chase Tower, just two blocks from the Esperson buildings, now ranks as Houston's tallest skyscraper at 75 floors and 1,002 feet.

1947

OLDEST THEATER COMPANY
ALLEY THEATRE
615 Texas Ave.

A brick-paved corridor led from Main Street to the back of a dance studio turned theater. That's how Houston's oldest theater company—and the third-oldest resident theater in the United States—got its name.

Nina (pronounced Nine-a) Vance, a former high school drama teacher directing plays at Houston's Jewish Community Center, got together with some actor friends with the idea to start their own theater. Vance purchased 214 postcards for a penny apiece and handwrote on each, "It's beginning! Do you want a new theater for Houston?"

More than 100 people responded. On October 7, 1947, the founding members of the Alley Theatre met in a dance studio on Main Street. This would become their first performance space, with opening night taking place on November 28.

The Alley Theatre originally seated just 87 people. During the first season, only two people were paid: the janitor and the office manager.

By 1949, the company had outgrown the space and relocated to a converted fan factory on Berry Street, where they performed until 1968. With donations from the Ford Foundation and Houston residents, the Alley Theatre debuted in its new,

$3.5-million facility in November 1968. Actress Maggie Smith was in attendance on opening night as an emissary from London's National Theatre.

Architect Ulrich Franzen designed the New Brutalist–style building, which includes two separate theaters that seat 800 and 300 people, respectively. Theatergoers pass through a tunnel entrance—a nod to the original, back-alley entranceway. The design netted the Alley Theatre the Honor Award from the American Institute of Architects in 1972.

The Tony Award–winning theater company has played in some 40 American cities, as well as internationally in destinations that include Berlin, Germany; Paris, France; and St. Petersburg, Russia. The Alley is home to a resident company of actors, which allows for up to 16 productions and some 500 performances each year.

The Alley Theatre is one of many performing arts venues in Houston's Theater District. This 17-block area features a total of 12,948 seats for live performances at flagship venues like Jones Hall, Hobby Center, Revention Music Center, and the Wortham Theater Center.

1955

OLDEST PERMANENT OPERA COMPANY
HOUSTON GRAND OPERA
510 Preston St.

Houstonians Elva Lobit, Edward Bing, and Charles Cockrell, along with German-born conductor Walter Herbert, formed Houston's first permanent opera company in August of 1955. (Herbert had previously served as the first general director of the New Orleans Opera). The first performance was staged the following January, with an inaugural season that featured *Salome* and *Madame Butterfly*.

Since then, the company has won a Tony Award, two Grammy Awards, and three Emmy Awards for its productions; as of this writing, it's the only opera company in the world to have won all three honors.

The Houston Grand Opera was the first in the United States to simulcast a live performance in 1955. It was among the first to use supertitles—translated lyrics projected above the stage for non-English performances—in 1984. And it premiered the world's first mariachi opera, *Cruzar la Cara de la Luna* (To Cross the Face of the Moon), in 2010.

The Houston Grand Opera presents six to eight productions each year at the Wortham Center (also home to the Houston Ballet). It's one of the only venues built after World War II constructed with the needs of an opera in mind. The 49-member Houston Grand Opera Orchestra accompanies all performances.

1969

Oldest Chinese Restaurant
China Garden
1602 Leeland St.

Marian "Mama" Jue opened the Chinese Food Products Company inside a former paint store on the east side of downtown in 1968. A year later, Jue's husband, David, who had gone to culinary school in Hong Kong where the pair met, decided to convert the shop into the China Garden restaurant. China Garden soon became *the* place to go for a business lunch over Chinese food.

Construction of a convention center hotel forced the business to relocate to its current location on Leeland Street in 1979, and loyal customers quickly followed. High-profile regulars included local attorney Rusty Hardin, late Houston Mayor Bob Lanier, and Houston Rockets radio broadcaster Jim Foley.

As you walk through the front door of China Garden into the dimly lit space, you can still see an original menu from the 1970s, complete with its 1970s prices. In the restaurant's early years, the menu included American fare like pork chops, hamburger steak, and fried shrimp, alongside Chinese offerings of fried rice and chow mein.

You won't find hamburger steak anywhere on the menu anymore. Instead, regulars swear by the lemon chicken, crackling soup (an off-menu favorite), and pork dumplings, along with

Cantonese specialties like egg foo young and chop suey. For a little taste of Texas, try the jalapeño shrimp.

Marian "Mama" Jue passed away in February 2021 of COVID-19, but her daughter Carol Jue-Churchill now carries on the family business. "My mother was a mother to everybody in Houston," Jue-Churchill said in a 2021 interview. "Everybody that came here, she loved to feed them."

China Garden is just around the corner from the Toyota Center, making it a popular spot for a pregame meal when the Rockets play at home.

—1978

Oldest Martin Luther King Day Parade in the United States
"Original" MLK Day Parade
Downtown Houston

D r. Martin Luther King Jr. was murdered while standing on his balcony at the Lorraine Motel in Memphis, Tennessee, on Thursday, April 4, 1968. The assassination sent the nation into shock. President Lyndon B. Johnson called for a national day of mourning, and the Academy Awards and numerous sporting events were postponed.

Two months earlier, while preaching from the pulpit of Ebenezer Baptist Church in Atlanta, King spoke of how he'd like to be eulogized, saying, "I'd like for somebody to say that day that Martin Luther King Jr. tried to give his life serving others."

Photo courtesy of the Black Heritage Society

Five years before President Ronald Reagan declared Martin Luther King Jr. Day a federal holiday in 1983, Houston became the first city in the United States to honor the Baptist minister and civil rights activist with a parade.

The first annual "Original" MLK Day Parade took place on January 21, 1978. It was an abnormally cold morning with ice on the roads and temperatures below freezing, so only a few marching bands made it to the event.

Also in attendance was Martin Luther King's father, Martin Luther "Daddy" King Sr., who commissioned the parade and served as its first grand marshal. Ovide Duncantell, longtime Houston activist and founder of the Houston Black Heritage Society, organized the first event. Duncantell passed away in 2018, but his brainchild continues as a beloved Houston tradition.

Photos courtesy of the Black Heritage Society

Now co-organized by the Houston Black Heritage Society and the City of Houston, the "Original" MLK Day Parade typically draws a crowd of some 20,000 attendees to downtown Houston. More than 130 parade entries take part, including marching bands, dance teams, military and ROTC groups, and first responders.

Houston is home to not one but two parades honoring Dr. Martin Luther King Jr. The "Original" MLK Day Parade takes place downtown, while the MLK Grande Parade marches through Midtown.

DOWNTOWN **31**

—1988
Oldest Art Car Parade in the World
Houston Art Car Parade
Downtown

While the art car may not have originated in Houston, it was Houston that first organized these moving visual masterpieces into a parade.

It all started in 1984, when local building supply company owners Kit and Carl Detering donated a 1967 Ford station wagon to The Orange Show Center for Visionary Art. This nonprofit foundation for the arts commissioned local artist Jackie Harris to transform the car. With a budget of $800 for paint and plastic fruit, the beat-up car became the Fruitmobile, one of Houston's first art cars.

In 1986, 20 floats and art cars cruised down Montrose Boulevard as part of the New Music Parade. That same year, the Fruitmobile, having been donated back to The Orange Show, took part along with 10 other art cars in a road show at The Orange Show Monument, a quirky folk art installation in Houston's East End.

The organizers of the Houston International Festival took notice and asked The Orange Show to organize a parade for the following year. In April of 1988, Roadside Attractions: The Art Car Parade took to the streets of Houston with 40 cars. The inaugural event proved wildly popular, and it doubled in size by 1989. Soon, art cars were caravanning from around the country to participate in the world's first art car parade.

Today, the Houston Art Car Parade Weekend comprises four days of festivities. More than 250 vehicles take part from 23 states, as well as Canada and Mexico. Anything on wheels can qualify as an art car, with past entrants including unicycles, lawnmowers, and golf carts. Some 300,000 spectators turn out for the parade, making it the largest free public event in Houston.

The Orange Show Center for Visionary Art operates several large-scale art projects around Houston, including The Orange Show Monument, neighboring mosaic-filled Smither Park, and Beer Can House (quite literally, a house covered in 50,000 aluminum beer cans). To see some art cars outside Parade Weekend, pay a visit to the Art Car Museum (nicknamed "Garage Mahal") in Montrose or Saint Arnold Brewing Company (known for its Art Car IPA and its collection of art cars on display).

West Inner Loop

1836

Oldest Cemetery
Founders Memorial Cemetery
1217 W. Dallas St.

Founders Memorial Cemetery, also known as the Old City Cemetery, serves as a rare anchor to Houston's early years—the first chapter in the book of Bayou City history. The two-acre plot in the Historic Fourth Ward was established as the city's first burial ground in 1836, the same year the city was founded.

In 1836, New York brothers John Kirby Allen and Augustus Chapman Allen purchased 6,642 acres along the shores of Buffalo Bayou for a new town for a little less than $10,000. The duo founded Houston on August 30 of the same year.

At the time of its founding, just a few months after Texas won its independence from Mexico, Houston was little more than a swamp shaded by sweet gum trees. The cemetery, now in the shadow of downtown skyscrapers, then was on the outskirts of town.

Many of Houston's earliest residents, including Houston founding father John Kirby Allen, who died of congestive fever, are interred within the cemetery. Most of the graves date to the 19th and early 20th centuries. The last burial at the cemetery took place in 1949. Victims of yellow fever, cholera, and smallpox outbreaks were sometimes buried in mass unmarked graves on the site, making it difficult to determine the exact number of those buried here. Conservative estimates put the count at around 850.

Famous figures laid to rest on the grounds include veterans of the Texas Revolution and officials of the Republic of Texas.

The cemetery also witnessed the first Masonic funeral held in Texas, when James Collinsworth, a signer of the Texas Declaration of Independence, was buried in 1838. Collinsworth had been running for the presidency of the Republic of Texas when, on July 11 after having a bit too much to drink, he jumped or fell off a boat in Galveston Bay and drowned.

Other prominent figures buried at the cemetery include Rebecca Lamar, mother of second president of the Republic of Texas Mirabeau B. Lamar, and John Austin Wharton, called the "keenest blade on the field of San Jacinto" after fighting in the battle that won Texas its independence.

Founders Memorial Cemetery sits next door to another historic burial ground, Beth Israel Cemetery (the oldest Jewish cemetery in the city). During the late 1860s, a community of formerly enslaved African Americans built a Freedmen's Town around the cemetery in what now is Houston's Fourth Ward. They also built Bethel Baptist Church in the 1890s; after a fire devastated the church in 2005, the City of Houston created Bethel Park around its four remaining walls. Learn more about Freedmen's Town at the Rutherford B. H. Yates Museum, two blocks south of the cemetery.

―――――――――――――――――――1866

Oldest Black Neighborhood
Freedmen's Town
Fourth Ward

After the Emancipation Proclamation in 1865, communities of freed slaves began forming across the South. These settlements, sometimes known as freedmen's towns or freedom colonies, often formed on flood-prone bottomlands near the edges of established towns and plantations.

In Houston, a community of formerly enslaved peoples formed their own Freedmen's Town on the swampy, inexpensive land along the southern edge of Buffalo Bayou, west of downtown. The influx of thousands of new Black residents brought with it the formation of the city's first Black churches, schools, and businesses. When the City of Houston refused to pave the neighborhood, residents purchased bricks and paved it themselves.

In the first decades of the 20th century, a majority of the city's Black professionals—lawyers, doctors, and businessmen—lived in this Fourth Ward neighborhood. By the 1920s, the population of Freedmen's Town accounted for a third of the total population of Houston. Blues legend B. B. King once referred to the jazz clubs and blues bars of the West Dallas Street entertainment district a "breeding ground" for musicians like Arnett Cobb and Sam (Lightnin') Hopkins.

*Photo courtesy of the
Carol M. Highsmith Archive*

The neighborhood began to decline in 1937 with the passage of new eminent domain laws in the Texas legislature. This allowed the city government to condemn or take over Black-owned properties to make way for highways and housing projects. The construction of Interstate 45 in 1955 displaced some 40,000 residents and cut off the Fourth Ward from downtown. Black homeowners began to move out of the neighborhood, and Freedmen's Town wouldn't see a cultural resurgence until the 2000s.

Freedmen's Town was added to the National Register of Historic Places in 1985, and on Juneteenth of 2021, this area known as the Harlem of the South was declared Houston's first Heritage District. This designation allows community organizations like the Houston Freedmen's Town Conservancy to lead preservation and beautification efforts on public land.

Freedmen's Town is part of the proposed Emancipation National Historic Trail. You can learn more about the neighborhood and its history at historic institutions like the Rutherford B. H. Yates Museum, African American Library at the Gregory School, and Antioch Missionary Baptist Church.

1871
Oldest Professionally Designed Cemetery
Glenwood Cemetery
2525 Washington Ave.

As cities throughout America began to grow during the 19th century, church cemeteries were filling up as well. One solution, proposed by the Massachusetts Horticultural Society in the 1820s, was the idea of creating a rural, garden-like cemetery at the edge of town. Mount Auburn Cemetery in Cambridge, Massachusetts, was founded in 1831 as the first garden cemetery.

The Houston Cemetery Company established the city's first professionally designed garden cemetery in 1871, with the earliest burials in 1872. This not only alleviated the issue of church cemeteries quickly becoming overcrowded with victims of yellow fever and other infectious diseases but also created a public gathering place and recreational area—a purpose many such garden cemeteries served at the time.

The cemetery was established on the northern banks of Buffalo Bayou beneath some of the largest live oak trees in Harris County. Instead of being laid out in a grid, the grounds here featured curving roadways, rolling topography, and views of downtown Houston.

In 1999, Glenwood Cemetery absorbed the nearby Washington Cemetery, bringing its total size to 88 acres. After a century and a half, Glenwood Cemetery remains one of Houston's most interesting (and expensive) resting places. A single plot can run anywhere from $8,500 to $50,000.

The list of interred reads like a who's who of Houston history and includes figures like the last president of the Republic of Texas Anson Jones, tycoon Howard Hughes, former Texas governor William P. Hobby, Kinkaid School founder Margaret Kinkaid, and Humble Oil Company cofounder Ross S. Sterling.

With its highly individualized plots; magnificent oaks, magnolias, and flowering crape myrtles; abundant wildlife; Gothic statuary; and extensive landscaping, Glenwood ranks among Houston's most beautiful parks and is a final resting place for some 25,000 Houstonians.

Glenwood Cemetery serves as the western edge of Old Sixth Ward along the Washington Corridor. Buffalo Bayou Park lies just to the south, with the Buffalo Bayou Park Cistern to the east near the Sabine Street Bridge.

1875
Oldest African American Cemetery
Olivewood Cemetery
1300 Court St.

This cemetery, on a bend of White Oak Bayou northwest of downtown Houston, shaded by oak, pecan, and elm trees, likely was used as a burial ground before Emancipation. Two headstones date to 1869 and 1871.

Richard Brock, one of the city's first Black aldermen, bought and incorporated the property in 1875, just 10 years after Emancipation. It's the oldest-known incorporated African American cemetery in the city.

The six-acre plot began as a Methodist cemetery with several hundred family plots. Today, archaeologists believe the graveyard has several hundred marked graves and as many as 4,000 unmarked graves.

The graves that are marked speak to the history of the Black community in post-Emancipation Houston. Notable community members interred at this United Nations Educational, Scientific and Cultural Organization (UNESCO) Site of Memory include Reverend Elias Dibble, the first pastor of Trinity United Methodist Church (the oldest African American church in the city); Frank Vance, who helped build Freedmen's Town and incorporate the cemetery; and Richard Brock himself.

Some epitaphs are more mysterious, like one that reads "Murdered Dec. 12, 1889."

Other notable features of the cemetery are the prominent burial traditions from West Africa. Some graves are marked with pipes, which signify a connection between the worlds of the living and the dead, as well as seashells, broken dishes, and mirrored or upside-down writing.

The last known burials took place in the 1960s. At the time, the plot wasn't owned by a church or the city, and it quickly became overgrown. The Descendants of Olivewood was founded in 2003 by descendants of those buried within the cemetery, with the mission to preserve and maintain this treasure trove of Houston history.

Olivewood Cemetery sits at the junction of the First and Sixth Wards alongside White Oak Bayou. Other historic cemeteries—Glenwood Cemetery, Washington Cemetery, and Founders Memorial Park—are all within a five-minute drive.

1874

Oldest Intact Neighborhood
Old Sixth Ward

Shortly after Houston was founded, it adopted a ward system similar to that of New York City. The city was divided into four wards that functioned much like voting districts, each with its own political representation. As the city grew, the Fifth Ward was carved from portions of the First and Third.

On April 18, 1874, the Sixth Ward separated from the Fourth to the south, becoming its own ward. This ward, today bounded by Washington Avenue to the north, Houston Avenue to the east, Memorial Drive to the south, and Glenwood Cemetery to the west, originally was part of John Austin's 1824 land grant.

During the late 1800s, the Houston Street railway extended along Washington Avenue. This brought businesses into the ward—boardinghouses, blacksmiths, saloons, grocery stores, and brickworks—and it became Houston's "uptown" for a time.

Many of the Sixth Ward's first residents were German immigrants who came to Houston in the 1870s. This community began building Victorian-style bungalows, many of which still stand today. In fact, the Old Sixth Ward has the largest concentration of Victorian houses in Houston.

While German immigrants were among the first to live in the Sixth Ward, they were followed at various times by Swedish, English, Irish, French, Swiss, Polish, Italian, Mexican, and Vietnamese immigrant communities.

By the 1970s, the ward was home to a predominantly Mexican American community who nicknamed the ward "Del Sesto." In 1978, it became the first National Register Historic District in Harris County. Thanks to this and later preservation efforts, many of the Sixth Ward's historic structures remain.

St. Joseph Catholic Church, built in 1901, still holds Mass in Spanish each Sunday (it's well worth coming for the mariachi Mass at the end of the day). Fire Station No. 6, now an office building, was built in 1903, and Dow Elementary School, now home to Multicultural Education and Counseling through the Arts, went up in 1912.

Famous residents have included Gwendolyn Zepeda, Houston's first poet laureate, and Mary Kay Ash, the founder of Mary Kay Cosmetics.

The shady, serene, and historic Glenwood Cemetery lies just to the west of the Old Sixth Ward. Within the neighborhood, you can pick up groceries, artisan items, or smoked barbecue at Henderson & Kane General Store, or see the original bricks of Houston's first brick-paved street along Sabine.

1883

Oldest Boot Maker
Maida's
3729 Westheimer Rd.

Salvatore "Sam" Maida, a 33-year-old shoemaker from Sicily, arrived in a fledgling Houston in 1883 and quickly went into business with J. C. Cuccia. At Maida & Cuccia in downtown, Maida made boots and shoes, and Cuccia cleaned shoes and washed clothes—a one-stop shop for working Houstonians.

Maida's son John already was apprenticing in the shoe shop when his father passed away in 1901. He took over the business, and soon saw an opportunity for a new service. Around the same time, boots and shoes had begun to be mass-produced in factories. No repair service existed at the time for ready-to-wear shoes, so, in 1906, John opened the Houston Shoe Hospital—a place where Houstonians could take their cheaper, mass-produced shoes for repair. This venture soon expanded to several locations around town.

These businesses have remained in the family for six generations. You still can take your shoes to the Houston Shoe Hospital for a fix, and you can still get a pair of boots handcrafted for your own feet using much of the same equipment and techniques that Maida's has been employing for more than a century.

A pair of custom boots from the oldest family-owned and continuously operating boot and shoe company in the United States takes an average of 65 hours to make. The staff at

Maida's hand-measures each customer's foot. Then proprietary technology scans each foot to produce an anatomically accurate 3D model (a newer addition to Maida's process). The resulting last—a foot-shaped mold used in custom shoemaking—makes a pair of Maida's boots among the most individualized available.

The Maida family has more than one venture in Houston. In 1990, John Maida's great-grandson Jason—a skilled leathercrafter in his own right—opened Maida's Belts & Buckles further west on Westheimer. You'll find nine Houston Shoe Hospital locations in the Houston area.

—————————————————1891
Oldest Suburb
Houston Heights
Heights Blvd.

O n May 5, 1891, the Omaha & South Texas Land Company purchased 1,756 acres of land west of Houston, 62 feet above sea level. They hoped the elevation—23 feet higher than downtown—would help prevent flooding and temper the yellow fever running rampant at the time.

The Houston Heights became the city's first suburb and one of the first planned communities in Texas. Among the men who developed it were "Father of the Houston Heights" Daniel Denton Cooley (grandfather of famed heart surgeon Dr. Denton Cooley), and company president and self-made millionaire Oscar Martin Carter, who moved to Houston to plan and manage a new utopian community.

Carter chose the area for its elevation, as well as for its sandy soil, mature trees, and rich vegetation. He envisioned an elegant community with a tree-lined esplanade, electric streetcars, schools, parks, and grand homes. Construction began in 1892. Carter developed the commercial strip along 19th Street and brought the first electric streetcar lines to Houston.

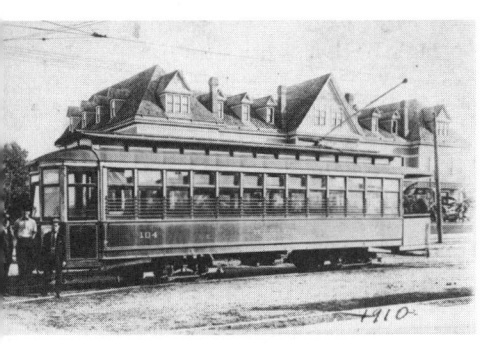

Photo courtesy of the Museum of Houston and the Houston Metropolitan Research Center

Photo courtesy of the Museum of Houston and the Houston Metropolitan Research Center

He laid out utilities and streets, including Heights Boulevard, which he modeled after Commonwealth Boulevard in Boston. The Houston Heights Hotel opened in 1892.

His 1893 home was among the first built in the neighborhood and served as a template for those that followed. The Victorian-style mansion featured luxuries like chandeliers and stained-glass windows, as well as more modern amenities for the turn of the 20th century, such as an intercom system.

More homes began filling up the neighborhood, with enough room for 24 homes on each residential block. Lots started at $250, making the Heights a relatively affordable place to live at the time.

The Heights incorporated in 1896 and was annexed by the city of Houston in 1918.

Much like many inner-city neighborhoods in the country, the Heights began a slow decline after World War II. Industrial businesses began moving in, and residents began moving out to the newer suburbs outside the city. By the 1970s, it had a reputation for poverty and crime. In 1973, a group of residents and business owners organized the Houston Heights Association to preserve, restore, and renew the neighborhood.

Since then, some 100 homes and buildings have been added to the National Register of Historic Places. It's now considered among the most desirable Inner Loop neighborhoods to live in.

While exploring the Heights, be sure to take a walk along the leafy Heights Boulevard pedestrian path, and do some shopping on historic 19th Street.

1899
Oldest Firehouse
Houston Fire Station No. 7
2403 Milam St.

When the Houston Fire Department became a fully paid, professional department in 1895, it got to work building the first firehouse, in what is Midtown today. The Romanesque building designed by Swedish-born architect Olle J. Lorehn was built in 1898 and went into service on January 18, 1899. It was active for the next 69 years, until its replacement in 1969.

Houston Fire Station No. 7—"Old 7's" for short—was built with two bays, one for a steamer and another for a hose wagon, each pulled by two horses. A watch office separated the two bays, and firefighters had a dormitory, showers, and lockers on the second floor, with three fire poles leading down to the bays. In the 1920s, the building was updated to make room for motorized vehicles.

Photo courtesy of Houston Fire Museum

The oldest still-standing firehouse in Houston now houses the Houston Fire Museum, founded in 1982. The collection features antique and modern firefighting equipment, as well as firefighter uniforms, photographs, emblems, and vehicles, (including a horse-drawn steam engine. One exhibit chronicles the 1947 Texas City disaster, one of the worst nonnuclear explosions and deadliest industrial accidents in our nation's history. All but one member of the Texas City Volunteer Fire Department were killed.

1902

Oldest Brick-Paved Street
Sabine Street
Old Sixth Ward

If you took a walk through the Old Sixth Ward in 1896, you'd be walking through dirt and mud. No roads in the neighborhood had yet been paved. That started to change at the turn of the 20th century, with the invention of vitrified bricks.

Cities around the country began paving their roads in brick—paved roads were a sign of a prosperous community. An article in the July 11, 1902, edition of the *Houston Chronicle* declared that "no city in the state of Texas can boast of being as well paved as Houston."

These bricks are heated at a much higher temperature to harden them and make them more impervious to water. They were first used in Charleston, West Virginia, in 1870. By 1898, Washington Avenue was paved in brick. Four years later, 1,809 feet of Sabine Street were laid with bricks.

Today, it's the oldest of six remaining brick-paved streets in Houston. And the unmarked bricks are not the only testament to the neighborhood's history. The Old Sixth Ward contains the largest concentration of Victorian and early 20th-century bungalow houses in the city.

Other brick streets have since been covered or replaced with asphalt. During phases of construction, it's possible to see the original bricks beneath streets like Washington Avenue and Heights Boulevard.

In other areas of the city, historic bricks are being returned to their original streets. In Freedmen's Town, 3,610 bricks originally laid by freed slaves were restored to the intersection at Genesee Street and Andrews Street in 2017. These bricks are among the only physical vestiges of self-funded construction by freed slaves and their ancestors within the city.

The Old Sixth Ward, located just west of downtown, is considered to be Houston's oldest intact neighborhood. Walk through the leafy neighborhood to appreciate the Victorian architecture, and stop at the old-fashioned Henderson & Kane General Store for locally sourced products and some of the city's best barbecue.

—————————————————1912
Oldest University
Rice University
6100 Main St.

R ice University was born from the murder of its namesake. Massachusetts-born William Marsh Rice moved to Houston after the panic of 1837 and began working as a merchant, supplying area settlers with goods imported from New York and New Orleans. His various business ventures, including sea freight, insurance, and real estate, netted Rice thousands of acres of land and a sizable fortune. He may have been the second-richest man in Texas by 1860.

In 1891, Rice decided to leave $200,000 of his wealth for the creation of an educational institution in Houston. The interest-bearing note would be payable to the Rice Institute for Literature, Science, and the Arts upon his death. Rice, a slave owner, stipulated that only White students should be permitted to attend.

On September 23, 1900, Rice was found dead in his apartment in New York City. His physician declared old age as the cause of death.

Instead of the money being released to fund the Rice Institute, his probated will directed that his fortune should go to his New York lawyer, Albert Patrick. His Houston-based attorney, James A. Baker, demanded an investigation. The investigation and "trial of the century" that followed uncovered that Rice's butler, Charles Jones, conspiring with Patrick, had chloroformed Rice to death to

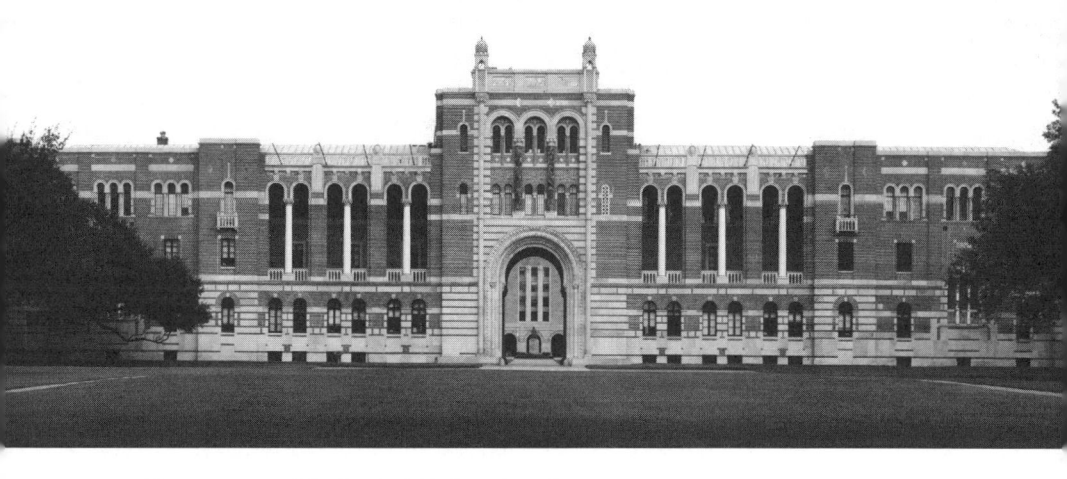

Photo courtesy of the Carol M. Highsmith Archive

collect on the forged will. Jones agreed to testify for the state, and Patrick was convicted of murder and sent to Sing Sing Prison, while Rice's original will was reinstated.

The William Marsh Rice Institute opened on September 23, 1912, on the anniversary of Rice's murder. Patrick was pardoned that same year. The first Black students would not be admitted to the university until 1963.

Since then, Rice University has grown from just 77 students in its first year to a total enrollment of some 7,500. Despite its sordid history, the school often ranks among the nation's top universities, its campus considered among the most beautiful.

> Rice University is across Main Street from Hermann Park, sandwiched between the Houston Medical Center and the Museum District. Rice Village, a popular shopping and dining district, sits just west of campus.

─────────────────1923

Oldest Local Fast-Food Chain
James Coney Island
3607 S. Shepherd Dr.

James Coney Island could just as easily have been Tom's Coney Island. Fate had other plans.

When Tom Papadakis arrived in Houston from his native Greece (via New York City), he had $75 to his name and a third-grade education. That didn't stop him from founding Houston's oldest fast-food chain with his brother James. The pair flipped a coin to decide the name of the unassuming hot dog stand in downtown Houston.

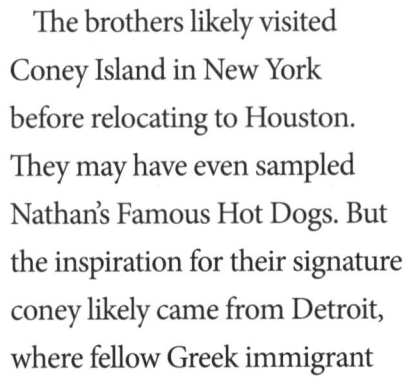

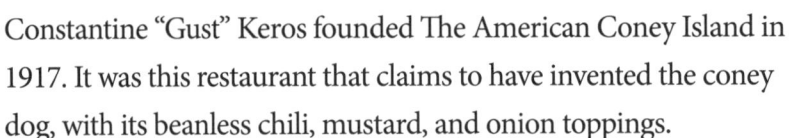

The brothers likely visited Coney Island in New York before relocating to Houston. They may have even sampled Nathan's Famous Hot Dogs. But the inspiration for their signature coney likely came from Detroit, where fellow Greek immigrant Constantine "Gust" Keros founded The American Coney Island in 1917. It was this restaurant that claims to have invented the coney dog, with its beanless chili, mustard, and onion toppings.

The original James Coney Island occupied the ground floor of the Beatty-West Building. The brothers cooked up a simple menu: hot dogs cost a nickel, and the secret recipe chili cost 15 cents. Back in the early days, you could also order a sandwich from the menu, including the then-popular goose liver and Roquefort cheese combination.

The Papadakis resisted the idea of expansion, and they didn't open their second shop for more than 40 years. The Town & Country Mall outpost opened its doors in 1968, and, by 1988, the company was selling some 30,000 hot dogs per day.

Six local Houstonians bought the company in 1990, hoping to save it from an outside corporate takeover when the Papadakis family was facing Chapter 11 bankruptcy. The original location shuttered in 1993, but the now-rebranded JCI Grill has since expanded to 16 locations around Houston.

The menu has expanded too. While you can still order the Original Coney—a wiener in a steamed bun with mustard, Coney Sauce, and onions—and chili made with the same family recipe, you'll also find a dozen or so other hot dog and topping combinations to sample.

JCI isn't the only place to feast on fast food that originated in the Lone Star State. Texas has been the birthplace of several other nationally known chains, including Whataburger (Corpus Christi), Taco Cabana (San Antonio), Schlotzsky's (Austin), and Jason's Deli (Beaumont).

———————————————1923

Oldest Outdoor Theater
Miller Outdoor Theatre
6000 Hermann Park Dr.

"To the Arts of Music, Poetry, Drama and Oratory, by which the striving spirit of man seeks to interpret the words of God. This theatre of the City of Houston is permanently dedicated."

These were the words written on the commemorative plaque on May 12, 1923, the day Miller Outdoor Theatre was dedicated.

When mining engineer and cotton broker Jesse Wright Miller passed away in 1919, he left his estate to the City of Houston. The city, unsure of how it could use the impractical plot of land, turned around and sold the property to Miller's sister for $50,000, and used the money to fund a permanent bandstand in Hermann Park.

Photo courtesy of Miller Outdoor Theatre

The original amphitheatre, among the oldest outdoor theaters in the country, featured 20 limestone Corinthian columns.

Each performance since the very first one has been free to the public and funded by the City of Houston—it's the largest free program of its kind in the US. The mayor appoints the Miller Theatre Advisory Board to organize performances.

Beginning in 1943, the City of Houston started allocating $5,000 each year to fund the Summer Symphony Series, which brings the Houston Symphony to the outdoor theater. Since 1978, a portion of the city's hotel and motel tax revenue has gone toward such programming.

Photo courtesy of Miller Outdoor Theatre

The theater has 1,705 seats (20 accessible to wheelchairs), as well as room for 4,500 more people in a grassy area for blankets and lawn chairs. The stage features an air-conditioned performance area and an orchestra pit that can be raised or lowered as needed.

The eight-month season brings an eclectic mix of performances to the stage, everything from symphonies and musicals to dance performances and operas. The venue also hosts the annual Festival Chicano.

Before or after a performance, be sure to enjoy the other attractions of Hermann Park, including the Houston Zoo, Hermann Park Railroad, Japanese Garden, McGovern Centennial Gardens, and the Houston Museum of Natural Science.

Photo courtesy of Miller Outdoor Theatre

1924

OLDEST MUSEUM
MUSEUM OF FINE ARTS, HOUSTON
1001 Bissonnet St.

The first spark that would grow into the Houston Museum District—a collection of 19 different institutions—began in 1900 when a group of five women began installing fine art reproductions in public classrooms around Houston. The Public School Art League, as it was called, was led by Emma Richardson Cherry, one of Houston's first professional female artists.

When the Public School Art League decided to establish a museum, it acquired a plot of land in the Montrose District, dedicating it on April 12, 1917. While fundraising for the museum stalled during World War I, the dream finally was realized when the museum campus finally opened to the public on April 12, 1924. Houston architect William Ward Watkin (who also worked on Rice University), built the structure, then called the Houston Art League. It was renamed the Museum of Fine Arts, Houston in the 1960s.

Original building, 1924. Photo courtesy of Woodson Research Center

Over the decades since its founding, the museum collection has continued to expand. Much of the early permanent collection came from donations by local philanthropists. One particularly notable patron was Ima Hogg. Hogg, known as the "First Lady of Texas," was an avid art collector. In 1957, she bequeathed her 28-room home, Bayou Bend, to the museum.

Today, the museum maintains a collection of some 70,000 works, spanning from antiquity to today. The oldest art museum in Texas also is one of the newest. The brand-new Nancy and Rich Kinder Building debuted on November 1, 2020. The space features site-specific commissions from several artists, as well as gallery space for displaying the museum's collection of modern and contemporary art.

At the time of writing, general admission is free on Thursdays.

The Museum of Fine Arts, Houston sits within Zone 3 of the Houston Museum District. It's within easy walking distance of both the Contemporary Arts Museum Houston and The Jung Center. Sprawling Hermann Park—home of the Houston Zoo, Museum of Natural Science, Children's Museum of Houston, and the Health Museum—sits catty-corner to the Museum of Fine Arts, Houston.

WEST INNER LOOP **59**

—1925

Oldest Statue
Sam Houston Monument
Hermann Park

Sam Houston stood tall in life—six feet two inches, if his military passport is to be believed. He continues to stand tall, not only in his namesake city's history but also at the Main Street entrance to Hermann Park.

A colossal bronze statue of General Sam Houston atop his horse, Saracen, has towered over the traffic circle just inside Hermann Park since August 16, 1925. The statue, arguably one of the most beloved pieces of civic art in the city, shows the general pointing toward the plains near the San Jacinto River, where he'd eventually defeat Mexican general Antonio Lopez de Santa Anna to win Texas its independence.

Landscape architect George Kessler proposed the monument as part of his 1916 plans for Hermann Park. The Woman's City Club of Houston raised funds for and commissioned the statue, and Italian-born sculptor Enrico Filiberto Cerrachio completed it in 1924 for a fee of $75,000. German-born stonecutter Frank Teich sculpted the granite arch supporting the piece. Four-year-old Margaret Bringhurst, great-granddaughter of Sam Houston, unveiled the statue before a watching crowd of some 3,000 people.

This likeness of the first president and first governor of Texas stands 20 feet tall. Cerrachio modeled it after Texan artist Stephen Seymour Thomas's painting, *General Sam Houston at San Jacinto*.

In 1996, the Houston Municipal Art Commission chose the monument as its first restoration project. That same year, a fifth-grade class at Bunker Hill Elementary School "adopted" the statue and raised funds through an annual raffle for the care and conservation of the Houston icon ever since.

Hermann Park isn't the only place to see a monument of Sam Houston. Drive along I-10 where it merges with I-45, and you'll see a giant bust of Houston (along with those of George Washington, Abraham Lincoln, and Stephen F. Austin) at American Statesmanship Park. Head north on I-45 to Huntsville, Texas, and you won't miss the 67-foot-tall statue of Houston standing above the treetops.

1926
OLDEST UNDERGROUND RESERVOIR
BUFFALO BAYOU PARK CISTERN
105 Sabine St.

When Kevin Shanley, a Houston landscape architect, stepped into an 87,500-square-foot decommissioned drinking water cistern for the first time, the unusual space reminded him of the ancient Roman Basilica Cistern near Istanbul. Roughly the size of 1.5 football fields, the space extended into the dark, its concrete roof supported by 221 columns, each 25 feet tall and reflecting in the remaining pools of water.

Photo courtesy of Katya Horner/ Slight Clutter Photography

Houston's first underground reservoir was built in 1926 as a drinking water storage tank and fire suppression measure for the City of Houston. It served its purpose until 2007, when it sprung an irreparable leak (maintenance workers couldn't find it) and was drained, decommissioned, and forgotten.

Forgotten, at least, until 2010, when the site was "rediscovered" during the $58 million Buffalo Bayou Park project. The City was looking to have the site demolished when the Buffalo Bayou Partnership stepped in to save it for use as a parking garage or for mulch storage.

When the project design team descended into the reservoir for the first time, what they found was deemed too beautiful to destroy.

"Basically, it's a cathedral of light and sound," Kevin Shanley said in a 2012 interview with the *Houston Chronicle*. "Can you imagine the right concert in here? Or art or sound installations? Different lights could change the look completely. Sometimes you might have water on the floor, but sometimes not."

His vision would soon become a reality. The Buffalo Bayou Partnership repurposed the space for large-scale art installations. It opened to the public in 2016, complete with a walkway that complies with the Americans with Disabilities Act (ADA) to make the singular attraction accessible to all.

Stepping into the space feels a bit like visiting a strange Gothic cathedral. Sound echoes through the cavernous chamber for a full 17 seconds.

To experience the cistern for yourself, book a 30-minute guided history tour or a multimedia art experience. The Buffalo Bayou Partnership also offers private tours and sound meditation sessions.

The cistern lies beneath The Water Works, a lawn and pavilion within Buffalo Bayou Park, just west of downtown. Pack a picnic lunch and enjoy the views of the downtown skyline, or do some people-watching at the free Lee and Joe Jamail Skatepark overlooking the bayou.

1927
OLDEST PUBLIC GARDEN
Bayou Bend Collection and Gardens
6003 Memorial Dr.

The 14-acre Bayou Bend estate was built in 1927 as the home of philanthropist, art collector, and "First Lady of Texas" Ima Hogg. Ima was the daughter of James Stephen "Big Jim" Hogg, attorney general and later governor of Texas.

Eight gardens surround the two-floor, 24-room Georgian mansion, landscaped into the natural woodlands along Buffalo Bayou. Hogg and her brothers Will and Mike chose the spot in the newly developed neighborhood of River Oaks. Ima began planning the gardens before construction began on the house.

According to Hogg, the area was "nothing but a dense thicket" when she began work in 1927. The formal gardens she designed were a nod to the Country Place Era of American landscape design. These gardens were meant to serve as outdoor rooms for entertaining, and many of them feel like natural extensions to the home itself. She planted camellias, magnolias, and crape myrtles, and many credit her with introducing azaleas to Houston.

In 1957, Hogg donated the estate and gardens to The Museum of Fine Arts, Houston, and the River Oaks Garden Club began supervising the gardens in 1961. Thanks to the club's work, Bayou Bend became the first formal public garden in the state to practice organic gardening. In 1966, the gardens and estate opened to the public.

Just across from Bayou Bend (sharing the same parking lot) is the Hogg Bird Sanctuary, a small natural area with hiking trails where it's possible to spot northern cardinals, blue jays, Carolina chickadees, and red-bellied woodpeckers, among others.

1929

Oldest Ice House
West Alabama Ice House
1919 W. Alabama St.

Before the 1940s, when electric refrigerators were rare or nonexistent in rural South Texas communities, Texans would purchase blocks of ice to keep their perishable foods cold in an ice box. Ice houses—precursors to the modern convenience store—got their start selling such ice. Along the way, some enterprising ice shop owners put two and two together and realized that maybe those same people buying ice might also want to pick up some cold beers. They might also want a stick of butter or a gallon of milk.

Soon, ice houses began selling other goods. Many homes didn't have air-conditioning, so communities began gathering at the local ice house for conversation over a cold drink. Each town had an ice house, and each ice house served as a communal living room of sorts.

West Alabama Ice House opened in 1929 when West Alabama Street was little more than a dirt road at the edge of town. Today, it's in the middle of the city. With the spread of the automobile in the 1950s, many ice houses converted to drive-ins and began pumping gas. Current owner Pete Markantonis's father, Jerry Markantonis, bought Houston's oldest ice house in the 1980s, when it was actually called the West Alabama Drive-in (Markantonis changed it back).

Nearly a century later, the West Alabama Ice House holds to its roots, serving only beer, wine, and soft drinks. But not everything has stayed the same. You'll find Texas and local craft beers alongside the Shiner and Lone Star, and cornhole and basketball have replaced shuffleboard and horseshoe. Families with strollers and groups of young college students rub elbows with the longtime regulars who come early to snag their favorite stools at the bar.

For the full "Walabama" experience, grab a spot at a picnic table, order a cold drink, and tuck into some of the famous barbacoa tacos from the Tacos Tierra Caliente food truck next door.

While many South Texas ice houses have shuttered over the years, Houston has held on to several. Bobcat Teddy's Ice House in the Heights took over the former historic Jimmy's Ice House. There's also Catty Corner Ice House in Garden Oaks, Kirby Ice House in Upper Kirby, and Sheffield's Ice House in southeast Houston. For a more modern take on the classic ice house, try a whiskey cocktail at Eight Row Flint.

1930s
OLDEST FISH MARKET
AIRLINE SEAFOOD
1841 Richmond Ave.

Airline Seafood opened in the 1930s along Airline Drive. George Theall purchased the market in 1948, and it's been in the Theall family ever since. Today, George's grandson Steve Berreth owns and operates the retail and wholesale operation, now located on Richmond Avenue.

Besides being Houston's oldest, Airline Seafood also ranks among the most prominent. Top restaurants, including Hugo's, Uchi, Weights and Measures, and Georgia James, source their fish here. It's also one of the only local markets with a federal permit to unload Gulf Coast seafood from boats directly onto its own trucks.

Airline Seafood sells fresh, largely wild-caught fish and seafood from both coasts, but the emphasis has always been on the bounty of the Gulf of Mexico.

Top chefs and local foodies come to Airline Seafood for local specialties like red snapper, crawfish, Gulf oysters, shrimp, and stone crab. Ready-to-eat offerings include fresh-made *campechana*, ceviche, and gumbo, as well as salmon smoked in-house.

Seafood lovers can pick up a fresh catch at the Richmond Avenue storefront or at the Urban Harvest Eastside Farmers Market each Saturday.

―――――――――――――――1930

Oldest Bakery
Moeller's Bakery
4201 Bellaire Blvd.

Goswin "Gus" Moeller and his brother Raymond learned the art of baking in New Braunfels, a town in the Texas Hill Country founded by German immigrants in 1845. After the brothers moved to Houston, they opened their own small bakery in 1930 on Almeda Road.

While the location of Houston's oldest family-owned bakery has changed twice since then, not much else has. Moeller's Bakery is now in its third generation, owned by Gus and Lucille's grandson Eric. The pre-World War II oven—a 1935 Middleby Marshall carousel oven—holds 18 sheet pans and is on just about 24 hours a day, seven days a week. Since the company no longer makes parts for it, repairs have to be done with custom-made parts.

Sweet treats are made fresh daily using many of the original recipes from 1930. Third-generation customers still come in to pick up their favorites, and many of the staffers have been working at Moeller's for decades—an average of 15 years each.

The bakery is best known for its delicate petit fours—rectangles of pillowy devil's-food chocolate or white cake topped with icing and delicate frosting flowers (one of many decorative options). You can also satisfy your sweet tooth with full cakes, pastries, cookies, pies, breads, and other seasonal items.

─────────────1935
OLDEST BBQ JOINT
PIZZITOLA'S BAR-B-CUE
1703 Shepherd Dr.

B arbecue might not be the first thing you imagine when you hear the word Pizzitola's. Houston's oldest pit barbecue joint didn't start out with such an Italian name. African American husband-and-wife team John and Leila Davis opened a small barbecue restaurant in 1935 under the name Shepherd Drive BBQ.

The pair smoked meats with hickory wood in two brick pits in their small back kitchen. In the early years, during the Jim Crow era of segregation, the Davises only served fellow Blacks in the sit-down restaurant. White customers had to go around to the back door to get their food to-go.

In the 1950s, when Interstate 10 was under construction, the Davises had to move their entire operation a few blocks south, literally taking down and rebuilding the barbecue pits, brick by brick.

Jerry Pizzitola visited the restaurant as a child—it was his favorite among the East Texas–style barbecue restaurants of the time. After John Davis passed away in 1983, Pizzitola bought the restaurant from the Davis family. He renamed the restaurant (with the blessing of the Davis family) but continued the tradition of slow-smoking barbecue in pits burning hickory wood.

Today, up-and-coming pitmaster Robert Quiroga oversees the pit room. The original brick pits are technically illegal but were grandfathered in. While you'll find brisket on the menu, it's the spareribs that stand out in true East Texas barbecue fashion. There's also a bit of Tex-Mex thrown in for good measure—chips and queso, barbecue tacos, and Frito pie topped with block-chopped brisket.

The Houston barbecue landscape is dominated by the East Texas style, known for specialties like pork ribs, boudin sausage, and a sweet, tomato-based sauce. To sample other styles, take a barbecue tour around town by trying Chicano 'cue at JQ's Tex Mex BBQ, Central Texas–style at Truth BBQ, Tennessee-style at Fainmous BBQ, Asian-Tex fusion at Blood Bros. BBQ, or Viet-Tex at Khói Barbecue.

—————————————————1935
OLDEST HARDWARE STORE
SOUTHLAND HARDWARE
1822 Westheimer Rd.

A bright-red and mustard-yellow mural painted across the side of Southland Hardware declares it "the store that has *almost* everything."

The distinctive smell of wood dust, house paint, and fertilizer, the mark of a hardware store, greets customers as they enter this family-owned business that's been serving the Montrose neighborhood since 1935.

Chester Gosnell first opened a hardware store on Almeda Road in 1935 before moving to Westheimer Road and eventually the current location. Arthur Voss, a former house painter, bought the store in 1962 and worked there until he was 80 years old. Marty O'Brien, who married Voss's daughter, took over when his father-in-law died at the age of 92.

The 16,500-square-foot space is packed floor to ceiling with tools, garden supplies, cleaning products, light bulbs, paints, varnishes, and a random assortment of gift items and knickknacks—in other words, almost everything. Items even hang from the rafters, making use of every bit of retail space.

The fact that this old-timey neighborhood shop has managed to survive the rise of big-box department stores is an impressive feat. Marty hopes that his own children will take over the store when he's ready to retire.

———————1936
Oldest Doughnut Shop
Shipley Do-Nuts
5200 N. Main St.

Lawrence Shipley Sr. developed his recipe for glazed doughnuts in 1936 and began selling them wholesale for a nickel per dozen. By the 1940s, the business was so successful that Shipley decided to expand into the retail market.

When Lawrence was out on deliveries, his wife Lillie would make doughnuts at the original location at 1417 Crockett Street. Each doughnut was cut by hand and served hot. This was an important detail to Lawrence Sr., who once said, "When they bite into that hot do-nut, it will bring them back every time."

His words proved true.

Lawrence Jr., who grew up making doughnuts, took over the family business and began opening doughnut shops across the South. His son, Lawrence III, took over from him. After becoming embroiled in legal battles over employee complaints of sexual harassment, discrimination, and failure to pay overtime, the company was sold to Austin-based Peak Rock Capital in 2021.

Today, Shipley Do-Nuts offers more than 60 varieties of doughnuts, as well as Texas-style kolaches, coffee cakes, beignets, cinnamon rolls, Danish, and apple fritters. The classic glazed doughnut remains the best seller, even after nearly a century.

1941
Oldest Cafeteria
Cleburne Cafeteria
3606 Bissonnet St.

The story of Houston's oldest cafeteria is a story of resiliency. This local favorite has twice been destroyed by fire, survived a big move, and has endured the COVID-19 pandemic, all the while serving the made-from-scratch comfort foods that have kept Houstonians coming back for more than 80 years.

It's also a story of the American dream.

Nick Mickelis immigrated to the United States from Patmos, Greece after serving in the Greek Navy during World War II. He arrived in Houston with a couple dollars in his pocket, knowing little English, and began washing dishes at his brother's restaurant.

Nick learned to cook and saved up enough money to open his own barbecue restaurant. His mother back in Greece had asked him to send her a photo. When he went to a local studio for a session, he had no idea that his photographer, Pat, would become his wife.

In 1952, Pat Mickelis noticed a cafeteria on Cleburne Street listed for sale in the newspaper. The couple purchased the Cleburne Cafeteria from Anabelle Collins and Martha Kavanaugh, who had opened the unassuming restaurant on May 8, 1941.

Nick had plans to turn the cafeteria into another barbecue restaurant, but as the story goes, the loyal clientele had other ideas. Despite never having eaten in a cafeteria before, Nick made the transition to the cafeteria business, keeping many of the same recipes from the original while adding some of his family favorites. The chicken and dumplings served on Tuesdays are made from the original 1941 recipe.

His efforts paid off. When Nick decided to relocate to the West University neighborhood in 1969, he and Pat handwrote letters to some 350 old customers. These loyal regulars showed up in a big way, making the reopening a grand success without the need for advertising.

The new location on Bissonnet Street has twice burned down and been rebuilt, and customers keep coming back. While other cafeterias around the country are shuttering, Cleburne continues to thrive. An estimated 70 percent of customers are regulars.

Nick and Pat's son, George, helms the restaurant these days.

"I was actually born upstairs above the cafeteria," George said in a 2020 interview. "My folks lived upstairs and worked downstairs."

He hopes his children will carry on the Mickelis family legacy.

The inner loop enclave of West University Place—home of Cleburne Cafeteria—is its own city completely enveloped by the city of Houston. Many of the city streets are named after famous writers, from William Shakespeare to Geoffrey Chaucer.

—1946

Oldest Fountain
Dolphin Fountain at Lamar Park
1419 Hyde Park Blvd.

Mirabeau B. Lamar, the second president of the Republic of Texas, kept a summer farm on the far western outskirts of Houston. It was on this land that Hyde Park was established in 1893. The neighborhood was annexed by the city in 1906 and today is considered central, just a few miles from downtown.

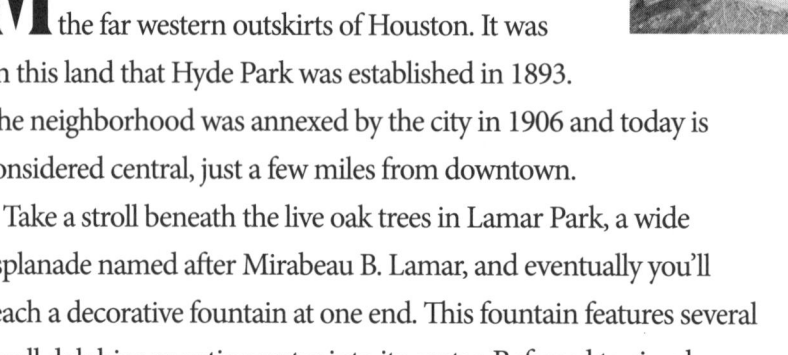

Take a stroll beneath the live oak trees in Lamar Park, a wide esplanade named after Mirabeau B. Lamar, and eventually you'll reach a decorative fountain at one end. This fountain features several small dolphins spouting water into its center. Referred to simply as the dolphin fountain, this feature was placed in the park in 1946 and is believed to be the city's oldest continuously operating water feature.

Seven decades of Texas summers and the usual wear and tear took its toll on the fountain. In 2013, the Hyde Park Civic Association launched the Dolphin Fountain Restoration Project to raise funds for a full restoration. As of this writing, fundraising efforts still are underway to improve the fountain (resurfacing the pool and replacing the plumbing system) and the surrounding pocket park.

The Hyde Park neighborhood has historical significance beyond its fountain as a key part of the LGTBQ+ community during the late 1970s and 1980s.

—————————————————————1947

Oldest Bar
Leon's Lounge
1006 McGowen St.

When Leon Yarborough came home from World War II, he purchased a bar and called it Leon's La Bomba after his service as a bombardier with the Flying Tigers in China.

Leon's Lounge, as it's now called, is the oldest bar in Houston to serve liquor from the get-go. It's housed in one of the city's oldest buildings (the oldest building with its original stained glass intact). Leon's was a true dive bar in those early days. Its namesake often would play poker upstairs with various Houston luminaries. At one point, he earned the nickname "Mayor of McGowen."

When Duane Bradley made an agreement to lease the space from Leon's daughter, Scarlett Yarborough, and reopen Leon's Lounge after a short closure in 2015, he envisioned returning it to the days when Leon himself was operating it.

"I went there when it was seedy and rough," Bradley told the *Houston Chronicle*. "It was a sketchy place back when I was going."

This Houston institution continues to quench thirst amid the lively Midtown party scene, serving classic cocktails and local craft beers on a black-and-white bar top beneath the dim light of its signature chandeliers. Photos of Leon and his wife adorn the walls. On most nights, Leon's hosts live music acts on the small stage in front of its backlit stained-glass windows.

West Inner Loop

―――――――――――――――――1952

OLDEST DELI
NIELSEN'S DELICATESSEN
4500 Richmond Ave.

Danish immigrants Vita and Niels opened their deli in Houston in 1952. The couple originally tried to sell *smørrebrød*, a traditional Danish open-faced sandwich typically eaten with a knife and fork. But customers trying to eat them like a typical American sandwich found them too messy.

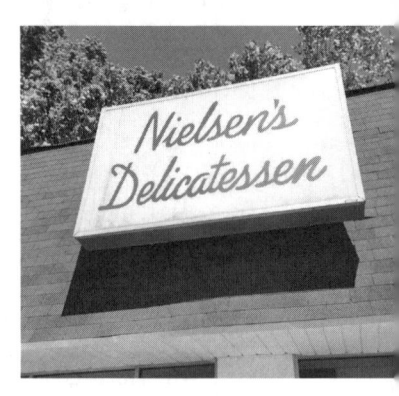

Soon Nielsen's Delicatessen made the switch to serving overstuffed, American-style sandwiches alongside coleslaw, potato salad, and Danish-style deviled eggs.

Not a lot has changed at the neighborhood deli since it first opened more than half a century ago. Third-generation owner Richard Anderson now runs the shop.

"When people come to Nielsen's they expect the same quality as it has always been," Anderson said in a 2016 interview with *My Table*. "They want to feel the same way they did when they walked in the very first time."

Locals flock to the no-frills deli for its homemade mayo, made fresh each day—you can buy a pint of it to take home with you. It's good enough that *Gourmet* magazine once requested the recipe after receiving an enthusiastic letter from a reader (unfortunately, it remains a closely guarded secret).

While you still can't get a *smørrebrød*, you can find traditional Danish items, like Havarti cheese and red cabbage (*Rødkål*).

1953
OLDEST GAY ORGANIZATION
THE DIANA FOUNDATION
P.O. Box 66523

Thursday, March 19, 1953, was a historic day for two reasons. It was the first time that the Academy Awards was broadcast on television, and it was the day that the first seeds for the Diana Foundation, America's oldest continuously active gay organization, were planted.

Houston florist David Moncrief loved the Academy Awards and loved to entertain. In celebration of the broadcast, he purchased a television and invited 10 friends to a pre-broadcast cocktail party at his apartment. The broadcast signal failed.

Undaunted, Moncrief tried again a year later, and, this time, he also bought a gag award to be given to one of his guests for the best "performance" over the past year. Moncrief's roommate had brought home a life-size plaster model of Diana, Roman goddess of the hunt, from the department store where he worked. Moncrief would decorate the statue when he entertained to make it feel like she was a part of the party.

On Thursday, March 25, 1954, Moncrief presented the first Diana Award.

As the event grew in popularity year after year, it moved from various members' living rooms, with baubles given as awards, to the Sheraton Hotel, Tower Theater, and eventually the Wortham Center. Tickets to the over-the-top staged performances, held on the Saturday closest to the Oscars, would sell out year after year. The highlight was the presentation of the Diana Award, given to an individual who'd gone above and beyond in service to the community.

In 1976, the Diana Foundation was granted 501(c)3 nonprofit status as a community support organization, as cases of acquired immunodeficiency syndrome (AIDS) rose. "The AIDS crisis nearly wiped out the organization," said Diana Foundation president Howard Huffstutler. Houston had few resources for those with HIV/AIDS at the time, so the Diana Foundation gave seed money to help establish the AIDS Foundation Houston, the Montrose Center, and various hospices to provide care and dignity for those living with HIV/AIDS.

Funds raised at the annual Diana Awards continue to be gifted to charitable, educational, and civic causes, most recently, the Law Harrington Senior Living Center. It's likely that the Diana Foundation has donated more than $2 million to the community.

While the Diana Foundation doesn't have a physical address, you can still experience Houston's thriving LGTBQIA+ culture in other places throughout the city. Most notable is Fairview Street in Montrose, with its concentration of gay bars and excellent restaurants.

1962
Oldest Tobacconist
The Briar Shoppe
2412 Times Blvd.

When Alice Amason founded her small tobacco shop in Rice Village in 1962, she turned more than a few heads. The single mother of two daughters recognized the unmet need for a larger variety of tobacco products in the local Houston community and decided to take matters into her own hands. As a woman in a male-dominated industry, Amason struggled to find a bank that would extend her a loan. She kept on until a longtime friend and customer, Richard "Racehorse" Haynes, lent her $500 to start her business.

Amason started small, claiming a bit of counter space in the Main Street pharmacy. But as time went on, she took over more and more of the pharmacy until she eventually took over the pharmacy's lease when the owner retired. The Briar Shoppe, Houston's oldest and largest tobacconist, was born. Amason's grandchildren, siblings Bill Scoggins and Diane Grace, now own The Briar Shoppe, carrying on its three-generation legacy.

While the store features a walk-in humidor and cigar accessories, it's primarily known for its pipe tobacco. The warm, spicy aromas greet you the moment you walk through the door. The shop's impressive collection of pipes hangs from the walls behind the counter. Keep an eye out for the ornate meerschaum pipe carved in the likeness of an eagle's talons clutching the tobacco bowl. It was Alice's pipe and is not for sale.

—————————————1965
Oldest Stadium
Astrodome
3 NRG Pkwy.

Few (if any) structures in Houston are as legendary and beloved as the Astrodome, dubbed the Eighth Wonder of the World.

Plans for a domed stadium already were in the works by 1960 in an attempt to lure a Major League Baseball (MLB) team to the city. Houston was awarded its MLB franchise on October 17, 1960, and construction on a new stadium began on January 3, 1962.

The Astrodome opened to great fanfare, both in Houston and beyond. The one-million-square-foot stadium was the first enclosed and air-conditioned sports stadium in the country. At the time of its completion, it boasted the largest clear span dome and the largest and longest scoreboard.

The 18-story dome was installed with Lucite skylights to allow natural light onto the grass playing field. What the designers didn't account for was how the afternoon light would blind the outfielders, making it nearly impossible to catch fly balls. Some of the skylights were painted over, killing the natural grass.

The solution? A new type of nylon turf was developed and installed in the stadium. This "ChemGrass" proved so successful that it became the standard for indoor stadiums across the country and was renamed Astroturf after its first home.

For the next four decades, it seemed like anything important that happened in Houston happened at the Astrodome.

Notable moments pepper the stadium's lineup of rodeos,

conventions, concerts, and events. Evel Knievel made a world-record-setting jump here in 1971. In 1973, Billie Jean King faced off with Bobby Riggs in the infamous "Battle of the Sexes" tennis match. And, 1992 brought the Republican National Convention to the Dome, which later provided shelter to displaced New Orleans residents in the aftermath of Hurricane Katrina.

Photo courtesy of the Carol M. Highsmith Archive

But time took its toll on the stadium. The Houston Oilers moved to Tennessee in 1996, and the Houston Astros played their final game in the Astrodome on October 9, 1999, before relocating to their new stadium downtown (now Minute Maid Park). The city of Houston closed the building in 2009 after a failed fire inspection.

"You and the people of Houston and Harris County have shown the world what men can accomplish when imagination, energy, and sheer determination are combined in one tremendous project," said President Lyndon B. Johnson after the opening of the Astrodome in 1965. "The Astrodome will stand as a deserved tribute to the genius of its planners."

After more than a decade of sitting vacant and facing the possibility of demolition, the Astrodome looks like it will continue to stand in tribute. The Harris County Commissioners Court recently approved a $105 million redevelopment plan to breathe new life into this architectural landmark.

Houston is home to six pro sports teams: the Astros (MLB), Texans (National Football League), Dynamo and Dash (Major League Soccer), Rockets (National Basketball Association), and the SaberCats (Major League Rugby).

─────────────────────1965
Oldest Sports Bar
Griff's Irish Pub
3416 Roseland St.

Griff's Irish Pub poured its first beer the same year the Houston Astros played their debut game at the Astrodome. It didn't take long for Michael Griffin's neighborhood bar to become a favorite gathering spot for fans of the Astros and the now-defunct Oilers and Mavericks.

Fans of amateur, college, and pro teams alike—collectively known as Griff's Army—turn out to cheer on their teams. When the Astros hit a home run, the Rockets win, or the Texans score a touchdown, celebrate with a free Jello shot.

You don't have to be a sports fan to appreciate Griff's, either. The bar also is home to the largest and longest-running St. Patrick's Day festival in Houston. Revelers turn out for live music, green beer, corned beef and cabbage, and a Houston favorite: boiled crawfish.

During the rest of the year, Griff's serves cold beers and hot bar food in a delightfully divey atmosphere.

As you walk through the front door, keep an eye out for the portrait of Janis Joplin on the wall. "She gave me the best advice I ever had," Griffin told CultureMap in a 2014 interview. "You gotta thank people, serve good food, and the third thing was, when they're leaving, you walk them to the door and thank them again. She told me if you treat people good, you may last 50 years."

Griff's has done that, and then some.

1965

OLDEST ITALIAN RESTAURANT
TONY'S RESTAURANT
3755 Richmond Ave.

While Italian immigrants have made a home in Houston since the 1800s, the Italian restaurant scene got off to a rather slow start in the Bayou City. Some of the region's oldest restaurants, like Gaido's Seafood Restaurant (1911) in Galveston and Massa's Oyster House (1944), were owned by Italian families but didn't serve Italian food.

The first full-service Italian restaurant, Del Monico's, opened in 1930, followed by a few others throughout the 1950s and early 1960s. But none had the staying power of Tony's, the oldest remaining Italian restaurant in Houston.

Tony Vallone opened a casual spaghetti house on Sage Road in 1965 when he was just 22 years old. The restaurant focused on the food and flavors of Naples—traditions he learned while helping his grandmother cook as a child in Houston's Third Ward.

Houstonians weren't used to eating authentic Italian food, and Tony struggled at times to get the ingredients he needed to recreate his favorite dishes. None of the seafood markets carried calamari, for example. He had to get it at a bait camp instead.

Gerald Hines, Tony's landlord, saw potential in the young chef and helped fund a move to the fancier Post Oak Boulevard, near the Galleria shopping complex. Hines nudged Tony away from the spaghetti house concept and toward fine dining. His investment paid off.

Tony's quickly became the place where Houston's elite came to see, be seen, and eat Neapolitan cuisine made from the best ingredients. *Houston Chronicle* society columnist Maxine Mesinger would write about the famous diners spotted at Tony's, a list that has included Zsa Zsa Gabor, Roger Moore, Princess Margaret, Mick Jagger, and every US president since Lyndon B. Johnson. Former president Richard Nixon once dined at Tony's with future president Donald Trump, and the late Italian president Francesco Cossigo once brought the G7 heads of state for a meal.

Tony's Restaurant is now located along Richmond Avenue, just behind Joel Osteen's famous Lakewood Church.

1972
Oldest Hindu Temple
ISKCON of Houston
1320 W. 34th St.

The passing of the Immigration and Naturalization Act of 1965 kicked off a large-scale wave of immigration from South Asia to the United States. A. C. Bhaktivedanta Swami Prabhupada, a spiritual teacher from Kolkata in West Bengal, came to the US on a mission in 1965 and founded the International Society for Krishna Consciousness (ISKCON), also known as the Hare Krishna movement, in 1966.

This branch of Hinduism, rooted in the Bengali bhakti yoga tradition dating back to the 16th century, took hold within the Western counterculture of the 1960s and quickly spread across the US and the world.

Houston's first Hindu temple was incorporated in 1972 in a home in the Montrose area as a temple for ISKCON. Two years later and again in 1984, the temple outgrew its location and moved to larger facilities, the latter a former church in the Garden Oaks neighborhood.

Services now take place in a grand mandir with gold-tipped domes, two terraced pyramids, marble floors, octagonal ceiling, and teakwood altar. The whole structure was modeled after the Jagannath temple in Puri, Odisha. The walls feature religious paintings of Krishna.

Everyone is welcome to attend services and events at the temple, one of 56 ISKCON centers in the country. Govinda's

Vegetarian Cuisine, the attached vegetarian restaurant (vegan on Wednesdays, Fridays, and Sundays), serves a buffet-style lunch and dinner prepared by husband-and-wife team Joynitai and Jamuna Dasadhikari.

Come on Sunday evenings for the weekly feast—an evening of chanting, dancing, and a lecture on the *Bhagavad Gita*.

Houston is home to some 120,000 Hindus and nearly 30 Hindu temples. Among the most architecturally stunning is the BAPS Shri Swaminarayan Mandir, a marble and limestone wonder in Stafford, Texas.

1974

OLDEST BOOKSTORE
BRAZOS BOOKSTORE
2421 Bissonnet St.

While Houston has had brick-and-mortar bookshops since the 1860s, the oldest still in operation dates to 1974. Karl Kilian opened Brazos Bookstore to support Houston's literary scene. It didn't take long for the shop to become a favorite gathering place for both writers and readers. The one-room store in West University started hosting readings by internationally known writers such as Susan Sontag, Ernest Gaines, and Martin Amis.

"I loved going to the events," Houston novelist Chris Cander told the *Houston Chronicle* in 2020. "Because as a poor student, I felt like I was touching greatness for the price of a signed book."

Brazos Bookstore wasn't Kilian's only vision for Houston. He also cofounded the literary arts nonprofit, Inprint, and organized the Houston chapter of PEN, a global association of writers. So big a figure was Kilian in Houston's literary scene that he was voted into the Texas Institute of Letters despite the fact that he was not, in fact, a writer.

Kilian made a move to the Menil Collection in 2006, putting the bookshop's future at risk. A group of 14 Houstonians—largely loyal customers—came together to purchase the shop. That group has since grown to 27 investors and co-owners, many of them prominent figures in the city's cultural scene. Kilian remained a loyal customer himself until his passing in December 2020.

As the rise of big-box bookstores and Amazon, plus the COVID-19 pandemic, forced many independent booksellers to shutter, Brazos Bookstore endured. The shop regularly hosts readings, sometimes multiple times a week. Despite its relatively small size, the shop seems to have something for everyone. Don't miss the wall of staff-curated books for top-notch recommendations for your next read.

For more retail therapy, head a few blocks south to Rice Village, a beloved shopping destination since the 1930s.

1975
Oldest Comic Shop
Third Planet Sci-Fi Superstore
2718 Southwest Fwy.

TJ Johnson started collecting comic books as a kid; his grandparents read these colorful, illustrated books to learn English after immigrating to Houston from Germany. After getting laid off from a job in the oil industry, TJ opened Third Planet in September 1975.

Much like the superheroes on the pages of his comics, TJ met with some resistance early on. Most notably, the Holiday Inn next door didn't love that TJ had painted his building "Captain America Blue." The hotel even offered to pay to have it painted a different color. TJ refused.

And when he moved his shop to its current location in 1988, it received that same signature paint job; the cerulean paint makes the shop hard to miss for anyone driving down Southwest Freeway. New controversy followed.

Third Planet now sits beneath a towering hotel. According to TJ, his shop has been bombarded with a stream of projectiles thrown from the neighboring building's fire escape. The onslaught escalated from ceramic mugs and crumpled cigarette boxes to a reported 14 metal fire extinguishers that punched holes in the roof in March 2019. Rain came through the ceiling and ruined some merchandise, and TJ decided to take action.

He filed a lawsuit against the hotel. His attorney, Cris Feldman, hired a team of illustrators—all longtime customers of the store—

to document the saga in comic book form. The 13-page comic was filed with the district court as part of an amended petition, making it an official part of the legal proceeding.

"I think it came together perfectly," Michael Brooks, one of the illustrators, told KTRK-TV, ABC 13 in a 2021 interview. "I thought this is kind of different because it has a lot of law lingo and laws embedded in the actual script, which is not how we usually do things."

Colorful litigation aside, Third Planet Sci-Fi Superstore remains the oldest independently owned comic book store in Houston and possibly in Texas. TJ maintains an inventory of some 520,000 unique items, including 70,000 new and vintage comic books in his showroom. It's a treasure trove of pop culture curios, covering nearly every inch of a space that smells to many like childhood.

Third Planet is on Southwest Freeway near Kirby Drive Pick up a comic or two, and then head a block north to Levy Park, a community green space with a dog park, splash pad, lawn games, and community garden.

―――――――――――――――1974

Oldest Crawfish Restaurant
Ragin' Cajun
4302 Richmond Ave.

Each spring, newspaper-covered picnic tables in Houston fill up with plastic-bib-wearing foodies tucking into piles of bright red crawfish, with some red potatoes, corn on the cob, and sausage thrown in for good measure. Fingers coated in Cajun seasoning pinch and twist, separating the head from the tail, peeling away the shell to reach the succulent white meat. The sounds of diners sucking the fiery juices from within the crustaceans' heads fill the air.

The tradition of a spring crawfish boil started in Acadian communities in the Atchafalaya Swamp in western Louisiana. Floodwaters would force mudbugs from their burrows, and local communities would celebrate with a feast. The season, which typically extends through March and April, coincides with Lent. French Catholics in Louisiana who forwent meat could still get their protein fix.

Crawfish season has the feel of a Houston tradition that's been around forever, but, in reality, it only emerged in the 1970s. Ray Hay's Cajun Poboys, a modest po'boy shop that opened in 1974, began hosting crawfish boils in its parking lot two years later. These springtime boils were a hit with the community of Louisiana transplants brought to Houston by the oil boom.

It wasn't long before Ray Hay's added crawfish to the menu; it was the first restaurant in Houston to do so. In 1981, the restaurant name changed to Ragin' Cajun in honor of the University of Louisiana at Lafayette Ragin' Cajuns. Owner Luke B. Mandola Sr. graduated from the school in 1972.

The popularity of crawfish continued to grow throughout the 1990s—the same time when Maryland was buying up Texas blue crab and driving up prices.

A larger-than-life crawfish sculpture towers above the entrance to Ragin' Cajun, welcoming diners who come to enjoy boiled and fried seafood, po'boys served on crusty French baguettes, and a slew of other Cajun specialties. Crawfish season kicks off in December at Ragin' Cajun, but the best time to eat them is from February to May, when the restaurant boils 10,000 to 15,000 pounds of crawfish each week.

The original Ragin' Cajun location on Richmond is just across I-610 from the Galleria mall. It's just down the street from Nielsen's Delicatessen, Houston's oldest deli.

1978

Oldest Vietnamese Restaurant
Mai's Restaurant
3403 Milam St.

The collapse of Saigon in 1975 brought the first major wave of Vietnamese immigrants to Houston. Attracted by the warm climate and fishable waters, Vietnamese refugees and immigrants continued to flow into the city throughout the '70s and '80s. Today, Houston is home to more than 80,000 Vietnamese and Vietnamese Americans, the largest population outside California.

Drive down Bellaire Boulevard and you'll see street signs in Vietnamese and strip malls packed with stellar Vietnamese restaurants and coffee shops. The flavors and ingredients brought over from Vietnam in the 1970s are now part of the fabric of Houston's culinary tapestry, and it all started across town at Mai's Restaurant.

Phon and Phac Nguyen opened the doors to Houston's oldest Vietnamese restaurant in 1978 as a way to provide for their family of eight children. The couple named the restaurant after their daughter, whose name means "golden flower"—a token of luck and prosperity in Vietnam. Mai went on to take over the restaurant in 1990 with a mission to take Vietnamese food beyond the bounds of Houston's Vietnamese community at the time.

These days, Mai's eldest daughter, Anna Pham, is the third-generation owner of the Midtown favorite, whose food Anthony Bourdain declared "some of the best Vietnamese in the country, if not the best" during his visit while filming *A Cook's Tour*. He once said he considered it his favorite place to eat in Houston.

Diners order from a menu packed with classic Vietnamese dishes—pho, fried rice, and vermicelli bowls—alongside more uniquely "Houston" offerings, like Vietnamese fajitas. This signature fusion dish features grilled pork, chicken, flank steak, shrimp, or fried tofu, served with cucumber, carrot, bean sprouts, lettuce, mint, cilantro, and rice paper for wrapping. It's topped with roasted peanuts, fried onions, and scallions for crunch.

For something a bit more traditional, try Mai's signature dish, *bo luc lac* (garlic beef). Chunks of marinated filet mignon are stir-fried with garlic, onion, bell pepper, and jalapeño, and served over a bed of lettuce and tomato with vinaigrette dressing.

Find Mai's in the heart of Midtown, just a few blocks southwest of Midtown Park. Come hungry, as the neighborhood is a hotbed of restaurants and bars. Houston's Vietnamese community has given rise to a beloved, uniquely Houstonian fusion food, Viet-Cajun-style crawfish. Try them at places like Crawfish & Noodles or Crawfish Cafe.

East Inner Loop

1865

OLDEST AFRICAN AMERICAN CHURCH
OLDEST AFRICAN AMERICAN CHURCH
TRINITY UNITED METHODIST CHURCH
2600 Holman St.

The Houston Methodist Church (now First Methodist Houston) organized in 1839 in the newly formed Republic of Texas. By 1843, the congregation had 68 members; nearly half were Black. In 1848, the church organized a mission for its free and enslaved members, with the Reverend Orceneth Fisher as its first pastor.

In 1851, the African Mission was moved to its own small frame building. In 1865, preacher David Elias Dibble organized the community into the Freedman Episcopal Methodist Church (later renamed Trinity United Methodist Church). The next year, the White members of the Houston Methodist Church deeded the frame church building to the newly formed congregation.

Dibble was born enslaved in Georgia and brought to Texas in 1837. He became the first Black ordained Methodist minister in Texas in 1864, the year before he became Freedman Episcopal Methodist Church's first pastor. Dibble would go on to become a trustee of the Gregory School, founder of the Mutual Aid Society, and member of the Most Worshipful Prince Hall Grand Lodge Free & Accepted Masons of Texas. He cofounded Olivewood

Cemetery, the city's oldest African American cemetery, where now he is interred.

The foundation for the first permanent sanctuary was laid on June 16, 1879. Since then, Trinity United Methodist Church has given rise to numerous Houston institutions, including other Black Methodist churches, Emancipation Park, Texas Southern University, and Wiley College.

The current sanctuary for Trinity United Methodist Church was built in 1951 and features a series of stunning, stained-glass windows that depict civil rights and religious scenes. Services are held each Sunday morning, and all are welcome.

Trinity United Methodist Church is in the Greater Third Ward, a short walk from Emancipation Park and not far from Texas Southern University.

————————————1872

OLDEST PARK
EMANCIPATION PARK
3018 Emancipation Ave.

F ounded by free slaves in 1872 to celebrate Juneteenth—the end of slavery—Emancipation Park in the historic Third Ward is the oldest public park in all of Texas. Baptist minister and former slave Reverend Jack Yates led the efforts to raise $1,000 to purchase 10 acres of land. They named the space Emancipation Park, a common choice for similar parks during this time.

The city acquired the park in 1916, and from 1922 to 1940 when segregation was the law of the land, it was the city's only park for African Americans. Ironically, the main street bordering the park was originally named after Confederate soldier Richard Dowling before being renamed Emancipation Avenue in 2017.

In its early days, the park featured a horse track and croquet courts, but when the Juneteenth celebration was later moved to Rosewood Park, Emancipation Park fell into disrepair.

That all changed in 2011, when a multimillion-dollar redevelopment of the Third Ward park was announced. The 10-acre space was rededicated in 2017, complete with a new recreation center and swimming pool, renovated community center and bathhouse, playground, tennis and basketball courts, and improved picnic areas.

Prominent African American architect Phil Freelon was the studio leader during the project, which won six American Institute of Architects and Urban Land Institute awards. Freelon's other notable works include the Smithsonian National Museum of African American History and Culture in Washington, DC; the National Center for Civil and Human Rights in Atlanta, Georgia; the Museum of the African Diaspora in San Francisco, California; and the Motown Museum in Detroit, Michigan.

The park is one of several Houston sites in the UNESCO Slave Route Project, and it's included in the planned 51-mile Emancipation Trail between Houston and Galveston.

Emancipation Park represents one piece of Houston's rich African American heritage. Learn more of the story by visiting Olivewood Cemetery (oldest African American cemetery), Antioch Missionary Baptist Church (oldest African American Baptist church), the African American Library at the Gregory School (first public school for African Americans), and the Buffalo Soldiers National Museum (which celebrates the contributions of African Americans in the military).

1908

Oldest 18-Hole Golf Course
Gus Wortham Park Golf Course
7000 Capitol St.

The story of the Gus Wortham Park Golf Course is not just the story of golf in Houston. It's also a story of resiliency and the power of community.

If it weren't for the efforts of Wortham Park Friends, a community organization founded to protect the park, the oldest continuously played 18-hole golf course in Texas might not be here today.

Founded in 1908 on the banks of Brays Bayou as the home of the Houston Country Club, the course hosted many golfing elites in its heyday, including resident professionals Tom MacNamara and Willie Maguire. When the Houston Country Club relocated from the East End to the upscale Tanglewood neighborhood in 1957, member and insurance magnate Gus Wortham purchased the course and renamed it the Houston Executive Club.

In 1972, the City of Houston purchased the course, naming it after Wortham. Over the following decades, it began a slow decline into disrepair. As the city struggled to fund maintenance of the municipal course, plans started to form to transform the space into a stadium for the professional soccer team, Houston Dynamo, or for the Houston Botanical Garden.

The Wortham Park Friends fought off these efforts, and, in 2015, the nonprofit Houston Golf Association secured a contract with the city to begin an $11 million revitalization of the course. The Gus Wortham Park Golf Course reopened for play in 2018 with a new Bermuda grass surface, irrigation lake, and a 300-yard driving range. Other improvements include a new clubhouse, grill, pro shop, and an educational space for the First Tee of Greater Houston program.

Today, golfers enjoy a 6,270-yard, par 72 course with views of downtown from several holes. When you're playing the 12th hole, keep an eye out for a brick-lined manhole filled in with greenery. According to local legend, "Howard's Hole" was the entrance to a secret tunnel connecting the course to the home of eccentric businessman, pilot, and golfing enthusiast Howard Hughes.

A two-mile hike-and-bike trail in Gus Wortham Park connects with the Brays Bayou Greenway, a 30-mile public green space that stretches all the way to Hermann Park and the Houston Museum District.

Photo courtesy Houston Metropolitan Research Center

―――――――――――――――――1941
Oldest Recording Studio
SugarHill Recording Studios
5626 Brock St.

Willie Nelson. Lil Wayne. The Rolling Stones. Freddy Fender. Beyoncé. Ted Nugent. J. P. "The Big Bopper" Richardson. No matter what music genres you gravitate to, chances are you've heard a song that was recorded at the oldest continuously operating recording studio in the United States.

The unassuming studio complex on a dead-end street in the Third Ward, built in and around the family home of its first owner, Bill Quinn, likely could not have existed elsewhere. Houston has no zoning laws—it's the largest city in the country that doesn't regulate land use, allowing land owners to develop just about whatever they want on private property.

Quinn embraced a similar "anything goes" policy when he opened his own independent recording studio under the name Quinn Recording in October 1941. At the time, Houston's postwar economy was booming, along with its population. The growth from 500,000 to 1.5 million residents by the early 1960s brought with it a thriving club scene for live music. Quinn offered the city's musicians, regardless of genre or race, a place to record their songs in hopes of producing the next big hit.

"Quinn was a 'Yankee' and started recording blues, Cajun and conjunto music when his southern peers ignored those genres," explained studio engineer Andy Bradley in a 2010 interview.

While the studio's slogan began as "King of the Hillbillies," its releases over its 80-year history have included country, old rock, zydeco, psychedelic, Tejano, R&B, gospel, Texas jazz, and contemporary pop. Memorabilia fills glass trophy cases in the lobby of the studio—a testament to its "no zoning" attitude.

The name has changed over the years, first to Gold Star Studios in the 1950s and then to SugarHill in the 1970s when it was purchased by Huey Purvis Meaux, but much has remained the same. The building still features parts of Quinn's original home, as well as much of his vintage recording equipment. And Houston's musicians—hopefuls and old favorites of myriad genres—continue to lay tracks within its historic walls.

SugarHill sits just south of the 30-mile Brays Bayou hike-and-bike trail between Bragg Park to the east and MacGregor Park to the west.

Oldest Soul Food Restaurant —1959
Houston This Is It Soul Food
2712 Blodgett St.

While driving around Freedman's Town in Houston's Fourth Ward in 1959, Mattie Jones spotted a frame house for sale at the intersection of Andrews and Buckner streets and declared, "This is it."

"This is what?" her husband Frank replied.

"This is where we're going to start our restaurant."

Frank and Mattie Jones opened This Is It Soul Food in 1959, serving lunch three days a week. This Is It served home-cooked soul food, inspired by the food Frank's mother made when she ran a Fourth Ward boardinghouse in the 1920s and early '30s, where the guest list included Louis Armstrong and Cab Calloway.

In 1982, the family relocated their restaurant to a larger location on West Gray Street. The movie *Jason's Lyric*, starring Jada Pinkett Smith, was filmed here in 1993. By 2008, This Is It had yet again outgrown its space, and, in 2010, the restaurant moved to its current location in the Third Ward.

Current owner Craig Joseph, grandson of the late Frank and Mattie, proudly declares This Is It "the best soul food this side of heaven." This hearty fare—ham hocks, black-eyed peas, oxtails, smothered pork chops, and chitterlings—originated from the food traditions of enslaved communities in the South.

These days, This Is It welcomes diners for lunch and dinner, serving meat and three (a meat dish and three vegetables, plus cornbread) cafeteria style. Come on a Friday or Saturday night for a live DJ, daiquiris, and hookah.

This Is It serves up soul food in the Greater Third Ward in south-central Houston, just east of Hermann Park and the Museum District. This Is It is one of many bastions of Black culture in the neighborhood. Diners line up around the block for a taste of fall-off-the-bone smoked turkey legs from Turkey Leg Hut or fill up on Caribbean fare (think jerk chicken and curry goat) at Reggae Hut. For East Texas–style barbecue, give Ray's Real Pit BBQ Shack a try.

1973

Oldest Fajita Restaurant
The Original Ninfa's on Navigation
2704 Navigation Blvd.

In the 1930s, a butcher in Premont, Texas, began referring to the cheap cut of beef that covers the diaphragm a "fajita." The term comes from the Spanish *faja*, meaning "girdle" or "strip." Even before the term was invented, this fajita, or "little strip," was often given to vaqueros (Mexican cowboys) as part of their pay, along with other undesirable cuts like tripe and cow head.

Tejano ranch hands in the Texas Rio Grande Valley created many dishes we'd now consider iconic from what they had available to them—dishes like menudo, barbacoa, and fajitas. During the 1940s, it became common practice to tenderize this tough cut of meat by pounding and marinating it in lime juice, and then cooking it on an open fire.

"Mama" Ninfa Rodriquez Laurenzo, herself born in the Rio Grande Valley in 1924, expanded her tortilla and pizza dough factory to include a small, 10-table Mexican restaurant in July of 1973. Ninfa's wasn't the first commercial operation to serve fajitas—that distinction goes to a fajita taco stand opened in Kyle, Texas, in 1969—but she is credited with popularizing chargrilled beef served in a warm tortilla. These tacos al carbón quickly became the restaurant's signature dish.

Diners can order them prewrapped in homemade flour tortillas (tacos al carbón) or sizzling on a cast-iron platter (fajitas).

Today, you'll find fajitas at just about every Tex-Mex restaurant around. Though the term has come to refer to any type of protein wrapped in a tortilla, a real fajita is always beef.

The Original Ninfa's sits along the Navigation Esplanade at the heart of the East End Mexican community. The East End Farmers Market takes over the pedestrian thoroughfare each Sunday. El Tiempo Cantina, a Houston Tex-Mex institution founded by Ninfa's son Roland Laurenzo, also has a location on Navigation.

1994
OLDEST CRAFT BREWERY
SAINT ARNOLD BREWING COMPANY
2000 Lyons Ave.

It's a hot summer day in the year 642 in the French city of Metz. Several local parishioners head into the mountains to retrieve the remains of their former bishop, Arnold of Metz. Covering difficult terrain with little to drink, the parishioners stop to pray for Blessed Arnold to intercede on their behalf. Almost instantly, their near-empty pot of beer miraculously fills up with sudsy liquid—enough to quench their thirst.

Thus goes the legend of Saint Arnold, Patron Saint of Brewers and the mascot of Texas's oldest craft brewery.

The more modern history of Saint Arnold Brewing Company dates to a Rice University dorm room in 1985, when Brock Wagner began experimenting with homebrewing. After a stint as an investment banker, Wagner decided to pursue his true passion and founded a brewery, along with his then-business partner, Kevin Bartol.

When Wagner and Bartol tapped their first keg of Amber Ale at The Ginger Man (a now-shuttered bar in Rice Village) in June of 1994, most Americans were not yet drinking craft beer. "The beer scene was mass domestic beers: Bud, Miller, Coors. Craft beer didn't exist as we know it today," Wagner said in a 2019 interview.

Houston also was the largest city in the country without a microbrewery. Despite a tough legal environment for breweries—Texas law did not allow them to sell beer directly to customers—Saint Arnold quickly outgrew its original location in northwest Houston. In 2010, Wagner relocated his brewery to a giant red brick building just off the freeway near downtown.

Wagner and his team transformed this former Houston Independent School District frozen food warehouse into a basilica of beer. When Texas began allowing breweries to sell beer for on-premise consumption in 2013, a change Wagner had helped lobby for, Saint Arnold began work on a sprawling beer garden overlooking downtown. This new space opened in 2018, along with a church-like restaurant featuring alcoves painted by Houston artists.

Today, the brewery remains a beloved institution where Houstonians come to quench their thirst beneath the painted gaze of Saint Arnold of Metz.

Until 2008, Saint Arnold remained the only craft brewery in Houston. These days, that number has exploded to more than 50. New kid on the block Local Group Brewing has its tap room just a few blocks away. A brewery tour of Bayou City wouldn't be complete without stops at Buffalo Bayou Brewing Co. in Sawyer Yards, Karbach Brewing Company in Spring Branch, 8th Wonder Brewery in East Downtown (EaDo), and Brash Brewing Co. in Independence Heights.

WEST AND SOUTHWEST

1854

Oldest Jewish Congregation in Texas
Congregation Beth Israel
5600 N. Braeswood Blvd.

The earliest Jewish families likely arrived in Texas with the first waves of European immigrants in the 1500s. Many of these early Jewish Texans were conversos—Jews who converted to Christianity, often by force, to avoid expulsion from Spain after the Alhambra Decree of 1492.

Spanish Catholic rule also crossed the Atlantic and into the New World. Until 1821, Spanish Catholic authorities in Texas made it illegal to openly practice the Jewish faith, though many of the area's early Sephardic Jewish families carried on their traditions in secret.

The oldest Jewish congregation in Texas got its start when a small community founded a Jewish cemetery on West Dallas Street in 1844 (today, it's the Beth Israel Cemetery). Ten years later, in 1854, 17 adults formed a congregation that met in a small room on Austin Street in downtown Houston. On December 28, 1859, the community received its charter for the Hebrew Congregation of the City of Houston.

A century ago, much of Houston's Jewish community centered around the area now occupied by the George R. Brown Convention Center and Discovery Green. As the oil boom and expansion of the ship channel brought waves of immigrants to

Houston, Congregation Beth Israel continued to grow.

By 1925, the congregation had outgrown its home and moved into a new synagogue on the corner of Holman and Austin Streets. Notable Texas architect and congregation member Joseph Finger designed the temple, which now serves as a performing arts venue for Houston Community College.

Congregation Beth Israel's current home in Meyerland, the new center of Houston's Jewish community, dates to 1967. The synagogue—today a Reform Jewish Congregation—serves some 1,600 member households and is one of more than 40 synagogues in the greater Houston area.

The residential neighborhood of Meyerland in southwest Houston is the center of Houston's Jewish community. Meyerland also is home to the Evelyn Rubenstein Jewish Community Center and Congregation Beth Yeshurun, as well as several smaller synagogues. While you're in the area, stop by New York Bagel Shop for some of the city's best bagels, lox, and schmear.

———————————1883
OLDEST HABERDASHERY
HAMILTON SHIRTS
5700 Richmond Ave.

Shortly after arriving in Houston in 1883, 21-year-old Edward Joseph Hamilton founded Hamilton & Scurry, a haberdashery offering "hats, caps, and gents furnishing goods." Notably missing from the early offerings of the oldest custom shirt business in the United States were, ironically, custom shirts. These would become a staple of the business.

Edward renamed his company Hamilton Bros. in 1886, and, by 1910, his younger siblings James Brooke, William, George, Bernard, and Arthur were all co-owners. The Hamilton family has continuously operated the business ever since. The script logo was taken from the contract Bernard Hamilton signed when selling a portion of the business to his son, Joseph.

Photo courtesy of Hamilton Shirts

Each client has their own paper pattern stored in a manila envelope for shirts that are truly custom. Cotton and silk fabrics come from the best mills in Italy and Switzerland. Every shirt is cut by hand with a single-bladed knife and sewn in the workshop, visible from the showroom on Richmond Avenue. In 1904, you could get a made-to-measure shirt for $6. Today, shirts start at $195 and come with a perfect fit guarantee.

Photo courtesy of Hamilton Shirts

David and Kelly Hamilton, siblings and fourth-generation co-owners of Hamilton Shirts, never felt pressured to continue the family business. But they did wonder if they could stay true to the success of three previous generations while evolving to cater to modern fashion trends.

"We shifted towards less formal because that's where the growth was," David told the *Houston Chronicle* in 2019. "It's been a long-term trend that accelerated after the financial crisis in 2008 and 2009. All of a sudden, nobody wanted to look like a banker."

The siblings also added a website and started accepting credit cards. Hamilton Shirts added its first women's line in 2018.

The Hamilton Shirts showroom, open by appointment, is not far from another hub of Houston fashion, the Galleria in Uptown.

1893
OLDEST WOMEN'S CLUB
THE WOMAN'S CLUB OF HOUSTON
5444 Westheimer Rd., #1425

In the mid-1800s, society still dictated that a woman's place was in the home, and women had few opportunities to pursue careers or education. That all began to change in the late 1860s, when women in cities like Boston and New York began defying social norms by organizing other middle-class women in their neighborhoods into voluntary social groups.

While many of these early women's clubs started out as social gatherings or book clubs, they quickly became a vehicle for social reform during the Progressive Era (1896 to 1932). They were involved in the temperance movement, suffrage, and with labor laws and civic issues that impacted women and children. They helped build kindergartens and establish libraries. And perhaps most importantly, they proved that there was power in numbers.

The Woman's Club of Houston, founded in 1893 on values of philanthropy, community, scholarship, and tradition, did similar work in the Bayou City. The club founded the first public kindergarten in Houston (and trained teachers to work there). It campaigned for the City of Houston to build the first public library and secured a $50,000 grant from Andrew Carnegie to fund construction. (The Houston Lyceum, founded in 1854, only allowed entry to White men.) In 1963, the club trained nearly 300 young women to care for children with cerebral palsy, which led to the founding of the Houston Chapter of the United Cerebral Palsy Association.

The charitable work continues today. The Woman's Club of Houston supports projects at Children's Memorial Hermann Hospital and has endowed scholarships for students studying urban education at the University of Houston.

The Woman's Club of Houston regularly meets in member homes and at venues around Houston. Visitors are welcome to attend but are asked to RSVP first.

1906
Oldest Independent, Nonparochial School
Kinkaid School
201 Kinkaid School Dr.

It was the early 1900s, and Margaret Hunter Kinkaid was getting married. The public schoolteacher learned that the public school system at the time prohibited married women. Instead of choosing between marriage and teaching, Kinkaid opened her own school in 1904 in the dining room of her house, in what is now Midtown. She had seven pupils.

After briefly closing for the birth of her son, the Kinkaid School opened officially in 1906. By the end of the decade, she was holding classes in nearly every room of her house. It was time for an upgrade.

Instead of moving the school into its own building, Kinkaid raised her house and added a new first floor. Even that became too restrictive by the early 1920s, with eight teachers and 125 students. Kinkaid helped form a board of trustees and tasked them with moving the school to a new facility on Richmond Avenue. In 1929, Kinkaid's son William joined as the principal and teacher of a newly added high school. In 1938, the first class of five girls graduated from the Kinkaid School and went to college.

Margaret and William served, respectively, as headmistress and principal of the school until they both retired in 1951. Margaret Kinkaid died in an automobile accident later that same year.

The Kinkaid School moved to its current location in the Memorial neighborhood in 1957, and the student population continued to expand from 884 students in 1958 to 1,466 pre-K through 12th-grade students and 143 full-time teachers today.

Notable former Kinkaid Falcons include George W., Jeb, and Laura Bush, as well as former White House chief of staff and secretary of state James A. Baker III.

The Kinkaid School is part of the Piney Point Village community, not far from the Houston Country Club. The neighborhood ranks among the wealthiest in Texas by per capita income.

1908
OLDEST COUNTRY CLUB
HOUSTON COUNTRY CLUB
1 Potomac Dr.

While officially chartered in 1908, the Houston Country Club's roots date to 1903. William M. Rice Jr. (also known as Will Rice, nephew of Rice University namesake William Marsh Rice) and some of his buddies organized the first golf club in Houston. They leased some land belonging to the Rice Institute west of town on the south side of Buffalo Bayou and laid out a nine-hole course.

Over the next five years, the club drummed up interest in the sport, prompting them to seek out a bigger and better site. A charter was issued on August 6, 1908, and the Houston Country Club was formed with Will Marsh as a charter member and its first president. By the end of August, the organization had 266 members. By November of the following year, that nearly doubled, to 497.

The club secured 156 heavily wooded acres southeast of downtown to develop an 18-hole course and build the first clubhouse. A. W. Pollard designed the Gus Wortham Golf Course, the oldest golf course in Houston.

In 1957, after nearly half a century at Gus Wortham, the club relocated to the wealthier Tanglewood neighborhood and hired renowned course designer Robert Trent Jones to build his first Houston course.

THE COUNTRY CLUB, HOUSTON, TEXAS.

Photo courtesy of University of Houston Digital Collections

Some significant figures have crossed paths while golfing at the Houston Country Club, some who may even have altered the course of history. George H. W. Bush played golf and tennis there, where he met James A. Baker III in the 1960s. Baker would go on to serve as Bush's secretary of state and White House chief of staff. It was also here that Bush met Robert Mosbacher, his future secretary of commerce.

The Houston Country Club is in the posh Tanglewood neighborhood, a short drive from Uptown, and The Galleria mall, and the sprawling Memorial Park, home to one of the top municipal golf courses in the nation.

1917

Oldest Restaurant
Christie's Seafood & Steaks
6029 Westheimer Rd.

Houston's oldest restaurant didn't actually get its start in Houston, but 50 miles to the southeast on the barrier island of Galveston.

Twenty-year-old Theodore Christie moved from his birthplace in Constantinople (now Istanbul) to the United States in 1905 and began working in the hotel and restaurant industry. Attracted by the tourism and gambling-fueled economy of Galveston, Christie made a move to the island, where he opened a sandwich shop inside the Tremont Hotel in 1917. His fried fish po'boy was an instant hit.

It wasn't until 1934 that Christie made his move to Houston, where he opened a series of full-service seafood restaurants. Business was booming, and Christie's was selling some 10,000 fish sandwiches each week.

James Priovolos and Steve Zoes, two cousins from Tripoli, noticed the crowded dining rooms one Sunday afternoon after church in 1963. The pair, having been advised that Christie's might be a good place to find some work, began bussing tables and seating guests. Christie, upon emerging from the kitchen, declared the pair a "godsend" in their native Greek. Just like that, the cousins were hired.

Fast forward to 1967. Theodore Christie was approaching retirement. Having no children of his own to pass on the

Christie's legacy, he offered to sell his restaurants to the cousins from Tripoli on the condition that they change their last names to Christie. Today, Priovolos's two children operate the last remaining Christie's location on Westheimer Road.

Diners still can order the famous fish sandwich from 1917, as well as a popular fried seafood platter introduced to the menu in 1934. Former president George H. W. Bush was a regular at Christie's, and he favored the oyster stew. Other guest favorites include the crawfish bisque, butterflied gulf shrimp, and whole flounder, served Greek-style with lemon, oregano, and olive oil.

The stretch of Westheimer Road between I-610 and Beltway 8 is packed with restaurants serving cuisines from around the globe. Come hungry.

─────────────1936
OLDEST BURGER JOINT
PRINCE'S HAMBURGERS
6600 Harbor Town Dr.

George Douglas Prince Jr.'s visit to the Texas State Fair in the 1920s would change the trajectory of his life. The former hat salesman was so inspired by the food prep at the annual event that he opened a small hamburger stand of his own in Dallas in 1929.

As automobiles were becoming more popular, so, too, was the concept of the carhop (a play on the name "bellhop"). The first carhops—fast-food restaurants where waiters would bring food out to people waiting in their cars—got their start in Dallas. Prince's was among the first.

Prince moved to Houston and opened Prince's Famous Hamburgers drive-in in 1936. Prince's burgers, fried on a grill in their own juices, took inspiration from a recipe Prince had picked up at the Texas State Fair.

America's growing love of car culture and teenage cruising, paired with popular items like burgers, fried shrimp, and open-face trout sandwiches, made Prince's a near-instant hit. His concept soon expanded to 19 drive-in locations around the state, recognizable for their carhops in band majorette uniforms.

Prince also was a natural showman, and he used it to fuel some of the most creative advertising the city had seen. He once landed an airplane on Main Street to order a burger. In the 1940s, he purchased a yacht and converted it into a restaurant location he called Yacht Hamburgers. Even his white Cadillac advertised his success with a bumper sticker that read, "Who Woulda Thought It, A Hamburger Bought It."

The beloved drive-in chain stayed in the family for two decades after Prince's death in 1966. After several closures, the franchise is making a comeback. Today, you'll find those same burgers at a small restaurant outfitted with original Prince's memorabilia at the Sharpstown Park Golf Course. The prices may have changed—you can't get a burger for 10 cents anymore—but the recipes haven't.

Prince's Hamburgers is in the clubhouse of the Sharpstown Park Golf Course, about halfway between Chinatown and the Mahatma Gandhi District. Harwin Drive a couple blocks north, is known for its bargain shopping.

──────────1941
Oldest Tex-Mex Restaurant
Molina's Cantina
7901 Westheimer Rd.

Every Houstonian has their favorite Tex-Mex joint—the place whose gooey, cheesy enchiladas they grew up with. Some families have been eating at Molina's Cantina for four generations.

Raul Molina moved from Laredo, Mexico, to Houston when he was 18 and began working as a busboy at the Old Monterrey Restaurant on West Gray Street. In 1941, Raul and his wife, Mary, purchased the restaurant and moved into a one-room apartment above the dining room.

Raul waited tables, the kids washed dishes and bussed tables, and Mary did the cooking. Much of the menu back then centered on a Tex-Mex staple: chile con carne. You could order the spicy ground beef stew on eggs, in a bowl, or smothered over a plate of enchiladas.

Many of Molina's original menu items—marked "Since 1941" on today's menu—still include chile con carne. But Raul Molina didn't invent the dish that gave birth to Tex-Mex cuisine. For that story, we have to travel west to San Antonio.

Tex-Mex cuisine was born from Tejano home cooking—the foods and flavors of Texans of Mexican descent.

In San Antonio in the 1880s, a group of Tejano women known as the Chili Queens started selling bowls of chili con carne in the city's public plazas. In those days, you could buy a bowl of chili with bread and a glass of water for 10 cents. By 1893, this Tex-Mex staple had made it all the way to the World's Fair in Chicago. Fairgoers could purchase the fiery stew from the San Antonio Chili Stand.

While the restaurant's name and location has changed over the decades, it has stayed in the family. Raul III, Ricardo, and Roberto, grandsons of Raul, co-own the three Molina's locations around Houston.

You'll find several other Houston Tex-Mex staples along the same stretch of Westheimer Road as the oldest Molina's location. These include El Patio, Ninfa's Mexican Cafe, Los Tios, and Chuy's (an Austin transplant).

Oldest Pizza Parlor
Antonio's Flying Pizza
2920 Hillcroft St.

―1971

Antonio Rosa was born in the small Sicilian port village of Pozzallo. After immigrating to New York at 18, he got a union job, but after going on strike for a wage increase of just a penny per hour, Rosa resolved to go into business for himself. He opened his first restaurant in the residential neighborhood of Mill Basin in Brooklyn in 1959. It was called PISA, and pizza sold for 15 cents a slice.

In 1971, Antonio and his wife, Rosalba, moved to Houston and opened Antonio's Flying Pizza and Italian Restaurant.

Hand-tossed, New York–style pizza is the star of the show. The vintage, animated neon sign out front shows a chef in a white hat and red scarf around his neck, hands outstretched, dough moving up and down. The sign wouldn't be allowed in Houston these days. According to Antonella Rosa, Antonio's daughter, their iconic sign was grandfathered in.

For many Houstonians, this is the pizza they grew up eating. There's a bit of magic in the animated neon sign and the spectacle of doughy discs flying through the air, the smell of yeasty crust permeating the cozy space, and Italian ballads playing softly in the background. With any luck, the Rosa family will stay in the business of flying pizzas for another 50 years.

—————————————————1986

Oldest Indian Restaurant
Raja Sweets
5667 Hillcroft St.

A display of bright orange, curly *jalebi*, India's version of the funnel cake, greets customers as they enter Raja Sweets, the first Indian restaurant to open in Houston and the longest-running Indian restaurant in Texas. Houstonians who've satisfied their sweet tooth with treats from the shop in the Mahatma Gandhi District (also known as Little India) for the past three decades have the weather to thank.

Joginder "Yogi" and Resham Gahunia, originally from Punjab, ran a restaurant in London for several years before fleeing the gloomy weather for the US. In 1979, they opened a restaurant in Cleveland called Front Row, but again, the weather was too frigid. Upon arrival in Houston, Yogi got a job as a manager at Burger King, while his wife, Resham, worked nights at Dunkin' Donuts.

After a few years, the family had saved up enough to open their own restaurant. They found a location in a strip mall in a non-Indian part of town. Yogi's motto was to "bring the streets of India to Hillcroft." He wanted to create a gathering place where the Indian community could come together, particularly during holidays like Diwali and Ramadan.

His plan worked. The Gahunia family founded not only the city's first Indian restaurant but also the entire Mahatma Gandhi District (the neighborhood received this designation in 2010). Other South Asian businesses began moving into the shopping center and nearby strip malls. Today, the neighborhood sits at the center of Houston's Indian, Pakistani, and Afghani communities.

Yogi passed away in 2002, and his daughter Sharan Gahunia now runs the shop. Everything—from the jalebi to the curries to the flaky, potato-filled samosas—is made from scratch.

"I would describe Raja Sweets as a walk-through India," Sharan said in a 2021 interview. "You can get North Indian food. You can get sweets from South India." And you can get almost 50 varieties of fresh sweets. *Gulab jamun*—milk balls in rose syrup—are a best seller.

The Mahatma Gandhi District is home to some 65 Indian and Pakistani businesses, including grocers, jewelry stores, sari shops, and restaurants.

South Side and Southeast

1927
Oldest Commercial Airport
William P. Hobby Airport
7800 Airport Blvd.

In 2019, the last year before the COVID-19 pandemic, nearly 60 million passengers passed through Houston's three airports.

That all started in 1927, when W. T. Carter Jr. built a landing field on a 600-acre pasture south of the city. The City of Houston purchased the airport in 1937 and named it the Houston Municipal Airport.

A year later, it was renamed the Howard R. Hughes Airport after the aviator's record-breaking flight around the world in July 1938. The name didn't last. It turned out that federal funding at the time couldn't be used for airports named after a living person, so the name reverted back before changing once more to William P. Hobby Airport after the late Texas governor in 1967.

As air traffic increased, it became clear that Houston was in need of a second airport. The Houston Intercontinental Airport (George Bush Intercontinental Airport today) opened on June 8, 1969, leaving Hobby to serve mostly private and corporate planes.

After a short slump, commercial carriers began returning to Hobby by the early 1970s. The newly formed Southwest Airlines began operating flights out of Hobby in 1971. Today, Southwest operates a majority of domestic and international flights from the

SOUTH SIDE AND SOUTHEAST 133

Photo courtesy of Houston Airport System

regional airport. Both Hobby and Bush airports have received a four-star rating from the international air transport rating organization Skytrax, making Houston the only city in the Western Hemisphere with two, four-star airports.

The airport's original Art Deco–style terminal was designed by Joseph Finger. It sat unused in the 1970s and since has been repurposed as the 1940 Air Terminal Museum. Exhibits tell the story of Houston's aviation history, including items from when the airport trained Women Airforce Service Pilots during World War II. The museum also hosts fly-ins, history presentations, and other cultural events.

Hobby Airport is in southeast Houston. If you have some time in the area pre- or post-flight, explore the 1940 Air Terminal Museum, grab some kolaches at the Original Kolache Shoppe, or take a stroll through the Houston Botanic Garden, which opened in 2020.

1948

Oldest Urban Expressway
Gulf Freeway

Construction on the first urban expressway in Texas began on October 1, 1948. Canadian-born William James Van London moved to Houston as a child and joined the Texas Highway Department in 1922. His vision to improve the city's poor road conditions included a novel idea at the time: overpasses.

When the first stretch of Van London's highway opened later that year between downtown and Telephone Road, Houstonians lined up to take a drive. The Gulf Freeway got its official name from a contest in which Miss Sara Yancy, a resident of the Houston Heights, won $100. But the overpasses, designed to ease traffic from train crossings, led motorists to nickname it "Van London's Rollercoaster."

Van London's Rollercoaster captured the attention of the Bureau of Public Roads (now the Federal Highway Administration) as a model to be emulated throughout the nation.

When that first urban expressway was completed in 1952, a crowd of some 5,000 people gathered on the Dickinson overpass, halfway between Houston and Galveston, to celebrate the occasion. The freeway since has grown into a 10-lane stretch of Interstate 45, linking downtown Houston with the Gulf coast.

Interstate 45 also ranks among the shortest interstates in the country, measuring just 285 miles.

Houston, for better or worse, now is known for its freeways, many of them a legacy of William James Van London. And that legacy extends beyond Houston asphalt. Van London's designs for a more utilitarian expressway (and his move away from the parkway ideal of the time) have become the standard across the country.

The Gulf Freeway heads southeast from downtown Houston and terminates on the far side of the Causeway Bridge on Galveston Island. Along the way, it passes through the smaller Texas communities of League City, La Marque, and Tiki Island.

1950s
Oldest Muslim Community
Masjid Warithuddeen Mohammed
6641 Bellfort Ave.

Houston is home to the largest Muslim population in Texas and one of the largest in the South. More than 100 mosques and centers across the city host communities from South Asia, Africa, Turkey, Spain, Pakistan, and the Middle East, and represent a diversity of Islamic sects.

The very first organized Muslim community originally held its meetings at Charlie Boyd's barbershop in downtown Houston. Under the leadership of the Honorable Elijah Muhammad, the community became a temple within the Nation of Islam, a religious and political organization organized in 1930 on a foundation of traditional Islamic and Black nationalist ideology.

During its early years, the community moved from location to location. In 1978, with funds donated by heavyweight boxer Muhammad Ali, the community purchased a former Christian Science Church and converted it into a masjid, or mosque.

After Elijah Muhammad's death in 1975, the community transitioned to Al-Islam and the teachings of Imam W. Deen Mohammed, a move away from Black nationalism and toward the global community of Islam.

Other mosques have grown from Masjid Warithuddeen Mohammed. The community also helped found the Muslim

American Cultural Association and Mercy Community Center, an outreach center that offers Arabic classes, prison outreach, interfaith dialogues, and orientations for new Muslims.

The community debuted a new mosque just before Ramadan in August 2010.

Masjid Warithuddeen Mohammed is in southeast Houston, down the street from Robert C. Steward Park and the Sims Bayou Greenway. Muslim centers are spread throughout Houston, but one of the largest is Al-Noor Mosque, near the Mahatma Gandhi District.

1951
Oldest Continuously Operating Opera Company
Gilbert and Sullivan Society of Houston
6127 Long Dr.

Over the course of a 25-year collaboration that started in 1871, dramatist W. S. Gilbert and composer Arthur Sullivan produced 14 operas. Many of them, particularly the comic operas like The *Pirates of Penzance* and *H.M.S. Pinafore*, became wildly popular across the English-speaking world.

In 1951, a group of friends united by their love of Gilbert and Sullivan came together to form what has become Houston's oldest continuously operating opera company. The group staged its first performance in July of 1952—*The Gondoliers*—at the Cullen Performance Hall at the University of Houston.

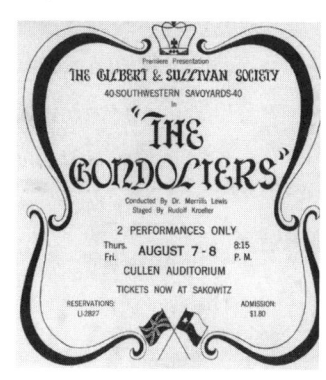

The Gondliers first show flyer, 1952. Photo courtesy of the Mary Metz Collection of The Gilbert and Sullivan Society of Houston

A *Houston Chronicle* reviewer liked it so much that he suggested the society stage a comic opera each year. Every summer since, the Gilbert and Sullivan Society of Houston has done just that, staging the touring repertory theater company American Savoyards at venues around the city.

The Gondoliers cast photo, 1956. Photo courtesy of the Mary Metz Collection of The Gilbert and Sullivan Society of Houston

In addition to being one of the city's oldest performing arts groups—only the Houston Symphony and the Alley Theatre are older—the society also is one of the few to rely almost entirely on volunteers. While the orchestra, musical and stage directors, and technical staff are paid professionals, the administrative staff and cast all are volunteers (including some professional singers).

The nonprofit theater company prides itself on providing entertainment for Houston families. In addition to setting aside tickets for less-privileged youth in the Houston area, the society also awards scholarships to students of vocal performance and theater tech.

The Savoyard Singers, formed in 2019 as the society's choral group, performs the music of Gilbert and Sullivan at events throughout the year.

In addition to its summer performances, typically held at venues in the Houston Theater District, the Gilbert and Sullivan Society of Houston also regularly hosts G&S sing-alongs at restaurants and bars around town.

1953

Oldest Public Television Station
KUHT
4343 Elgin St.

On May 25, 1953, KUHT signed on as America's first public television station, predating both the Corporation for Public Broadcasting (CPB) and the Public Broadcasting System (PBS). The station, broadcast on Channel 8 from the remodeled radio studios of the University of Houston's Ezekiel W. Cullen Building, was only the second television station in Houston.

The vision began in 1951, when University of Houston (UH) president Dr. Walter Kemmerer first proposed the station. UH already had launched the country's first university-licensed radio station the year before, and Kemmerer wanted to expand the university's classroom offerings even further.

UH applied with the Federal Communications Commission (FCC) on April 17, 1951, and went on air just over a month later.

"With television, the walls of the classroom disappear," said FCC commissioner Frieda Hennock in her speech at KUHT's dedication ceremony. "Every set within viewing range of the signal is a potential classroom."

The first week of programming included shows entitled *Bookland*, *Experiment in Teaching*, *Jack Armistead's Music Show*, and *Spring Quarterback*, along with 15-minute newscasts. Other early programming included credit courses taught on TV, like

Psychology 231, taught by Dr. Richard I. Evans.

And the television station continued to experiment and innovate. It broadcast in color for the first time in 1964 and became the first TV station in the country to telecast with closed captioning for the hearing impaired in 1981. In 1991, KUHT was the first station in the country to offer bilingual capabilities and descriptive video for those with visual impairments.

KUHT-TV 8 broadcasts from the Third Ward near the University of Houston main campus. Houston Public Media, which operates the station, also provides free content through its radio station, KUHF-News 88.7.

1956
Oldest Kolache Shop
The Original Kolache Shoppe
5404 Telephone Rd.

The *kolache*, a beloved pastry across many parts of Texas, was brought to the Lone Star State by Czechs who settled across Central Texas before the Civil War.

In those early days, the sweet pastries were homemade and stuffed with common Eastern European ingredients—apricots, prunes, cherries, or poppy seeds. Each family had its own recipe. Commercial kolache bakeries didn't start showing up on the Texas culinary map until the 1950s.

In 1956, just four years after the first Czech bakery in the state opened in the town of West, Lorraine Sharp opened her own bakery in southeast Houston, using family recipes. Today, Lorraine's grandson Kevin Dowd continues the family tradition.

Locals line up, sometimes before the sun rises, for The Original Kolache Shoppe's pillowy, yeasty, and stretchy kolaches, made from scratch daily.

"Traditionally, a kolache is a fruit-filled pastry," explained Dowd in a HighDrive Network interview. "You'll have a dollop of fruit in the middle. On the outside, you're going to have a puffy ring of supple dough."

Equally popular are the savory cousins to the kolache, the *klobasnek*—a Czech pastry traditionally stuffed with kielbasa sausage. While Dowd has continued to serve traditional favorites, he hasn't shied away from innovation, either. New additions to The Original Kolache Shoppe include a coffee program using beans from Dowd's own roastery, Zeppelin Coffee, as well as a popular menu of stuffed croissants baked with house-made phyllo dough.

While you should certainly sample the traditional fruit-filled kolaches, don't miss the sausage, jalapeño, and cheese klobasnek—a Tejano take on the Czech classic.

The Original Kolache Shoppe's location on the south side makes it a convenient breakfast stop on the way to or from nearby Hobby Airport.

1988
OLDEST BUDDHIST TEMPLE
HOUSTON BUDDHIST VIHARA
8727 Radio Rd.

Buddhism first came to the United States with Chinese immigrants in the mid-19th century. Japanese communities began establishing themselves on the West Coast starting in 1880, and by the turn of the 20th century, they'd established temples along the coast, from Mexico to Canada.

While there was curiosity about Buddhism during the Victorian era, its practice remained largely confined to Asian communities that had immigrated to the Americas. This began to change in the 1930s, when the books and lectures of Daisetsu Teitaro Suzuki introduced many non-Asian Westerners to Zen Buddhism. Beat Generation writers like Allen Ginsberg and Jack Kerouac continued to popularize Zen throughout the 1950s and 1960s.

The lifting of harsh immigration laws in the 1960s brought in a new wave of immigration from Southeast Asia and Sri Lanka, along with a renewed, growing interest in other schools of Buddhism.

While the first Buddhist organization in Houston, the Texas Buddhist Association, was founded in 1979, the oldest extant Buddhist temple in the city was founded in June 1988 by Sri Lankan monks, the Venerable Pannila Ananda and the Venerable Walpola Piyananda, who'd previously established a temple in Los Angeles in 1975. The pair founded a temple in Houston under the Attanagalla Raja Maha Viharaya temple in western Sri Lanka.

A new temple building opened in 2000, followed by the installment of a stupa and the planting of a Bodhi tree—the type of sacred fig tree under which the Buddha sat when he attained enlightenment.

The Houston Buddhist Vihara practices Theravada Buddhism, considered the oldest existing school of Buddhism, and a school commonly practiced across Southeast Asia. It's also the official religion of Sri Lanka.

Today, it's the largest Sri Lankan Buddhist temple in Texas, with some 400 people attending services. The grounds include a great hall, dining hall, and residences for monks, as well as a meditation garden and a playground. Temple programming features meditation classes, summer writing workshops for kids, and annual Sri Lankan New Year and Independence Day celebrations.

Houston Buddhist Vihara sits near Hobby Airport in southeast Houston. Just across I-45, you'll find another Buddhist temple, the Phật Quang Vietnamese Buddhist Pagoda.

Treasures Outside the City

1822
Oldest Operating Ferry
Lynchburg Ferry
1001 Independence Pkwy. N., Baytown, TX

The oldest continuously operating ferry service in Texas predates the founding of Houston.

In 1822, Nathanial Lynch started a ferry service, then known as Lynch's Ferry, on the San Jacinto River just below its confluence with Buffalo Bayou. At the time, this crossing fell along a main land route between South Texas and the Mexican border. The original ferry comprised a flatboat and a hand-pulled rope. During Santa Anna's attempted conquest of Texas in 1836, some 5,000 fleeing residents used the ferry on their escape route to Louisiana, some waiting days to board.

Lynch bequeathed the ferry to his family, who operated it until 1848. After passing through the hands of a series of operators, it was taken over by Harris County and renamed the Lynchburg Ferry. It's been free since 1888.

Photo courtesy of the Carol M. Highsmith Archive

Today, the Lynchburg Ferry crosses the Houston Ship Channel, connecting North and South Independence Parkway and the San Jacinto Battleground Monument. The William P. Hobby and Ross S. Sterling ferryboats, built in 1964 and named after former Texas governors, can ferry pedestrians, bicycles, and up to 10 vehicles apiece. The crossing takes 5 to 10 minutes, depending on wind and currents.

1826

OLDEST TOWN IN HARRIS COUNTY
HARRISBURG

I f history had gone just a bit differently, the suburb of Harrisburg east of downtown might have become the nation's fourth-largest city, instead of Houston.

In 1826, 15 years before the founding of Houston at Allen's Landing, New York-born entrepreneur John Richardson Harris founded Harrisburg at the confluence of Brays and Buffalo Bayous. He opened a store, sawmill, and gristmill and named the town after himself and Harrisburg, Pennsylvania, which had been founded by and named for his great-grandfather.

By 1833, the town had grown into the main port for freight and for immigrants in Mexican Texas traveling to the communities of the upper Brazos River. In March of 1936, Harrisburg even became the third capital of the Republic of Texas, but that's when things took a turn for the worse.

The Mexican Army under command of General Santa Ana torched the town within days of it becoming the capital. The seat of the Republic soon relocated to Galveston (and later Houston, then Austin), while Harrisburg was left to rebuild.

And rebuild it did. On September 7, 1853, Harrisburg became the first railroad terminal in Texas when the Buffalo Bayou, Brazos, and Colorado railroad opened its first stretch of track. But when the railroad relocated to Houston in 1870, the town began to decline.

Houston annexed Harrisburg in 1926.

This suburb east of downtown, unknown even to many native Houstonians, is a hub of Houston's Mexican American community. Take a stroll through Old Town Harrisburg for a sense of what the town might have been like in its early days.

The last vestige of the original town of Harrisburg is the Glendale Cemetery, established by John Richardson Harris as a private burial plot for his family members. The cemetery overlooks the Houston Ship Channel.

―――――――――――――――――1842

OLDEST NEWSPAPER IN TEXAS
THE DAILY NEWS
8522 Teichman Rd., Galveston, TX

"STORY OF THE GREAT DISASTER AT GALVESTON"
"JAPAN ATTACKS U.S. IN PACIFIC"
"MAN LANDS, TAKES FIRST MOON WALK"

The oldest continuously published paper in Texas has covered its fair share of state and national history since its first issue went to print on April 11, 1842.

George French published the first issue of *The Daily News* using a cast-iron handpress on a single sheet of paper. At the time, it was one of nearly 20 newspapers competing for the attention of Galveston's 4,000 residents. Texas was its own republic, and Sam Houston was president. A copy of the paper cost 6.5 cents.

You still can see the original R. Hoe & Co.'s Washington Press No. 2369 in the lobby of *The Daily News* in Galveston, just south of Houston. The press was originally used to print the *San Luis Advocate*, a paper that went under within its first year. On its way to its new home in Galveston, the press met tragedy when the schooner carrying it

TREASURES OUTSIDE THE CITY **151**

capsized. After spending several months in the bottom of West Bay, the press was retrieved, restored, and sold to Samuel Bangs, brother-in-law of publisher George French.

By 1855, the handpress had been replaced by a more efficient printing press powered by a horse or mule treading a mill. Production moved to Houston for a brief period during the Civil War, when Union troops occupied the island, before returning to Galveston in 1866. In 1885, *The Dallas Morning News* launched as a satellite publication.

Photo courtesy of the Library of Congress

The history of the paper is a history of firsts: first (and only) newspaper published under three flags (Republic of Texas, Confederate States, and United States), first building in the country purpose-built for a newspaper, first telephone connection in Texas, first newspaper with a dedicated train to circulate its papers, and first newspaper to publish a report sent by telegraph.

Photo courtesy of the Abilene Library Consortium

The Daily News building sits just across the Galveston Causeway from the mainland on a peninsula between Offatts Bayou and West Bay

---

OLDEST BUSINES IN TEXAS
IMPERIAL SUGAR CO.
3 Sugar Creek Center Blvd., Sugar Land, TX

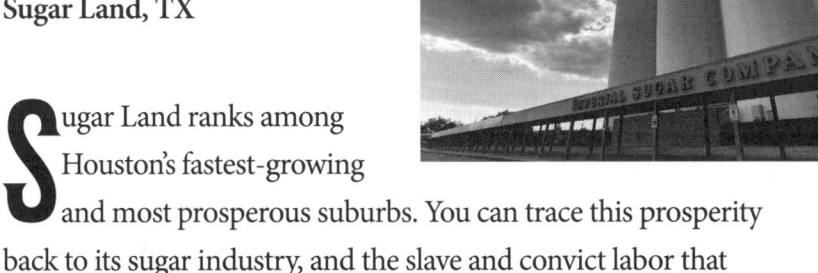

———1843

Sugar Land ranks among Houston's fastest-growing and most prosperous suburbs. You can trace this prosperity back to its sugar industry, and the slave and convict labor that fueled it during the late 19th and early 20th centuries.

In 1840, after the fight for Independence from Mexico, Stephen F. Austin granted his assistant Samuel May Williams a swath of land in what now is present-day Sugar Land. Samuel and his brothers Nathaniel and Matthew built mule-powered mills on the banks of Oyster Creek and began grinding sugarcane, using the labor of enslaved people.

In 1943, the brothers opened a commercial sugar mill, what would become the Imperial Sugar Company—the oldest extant business in Texas.

The company changed ownership several times in its first decades, all while practicing a series of unethical labor practices. After slavery was abolished in the late 1880s, Imperial Sugar Company turned to convict leasing as a source for cheap labor, at one point leasing the entire population of the Texas prison system. Harvesting often was more arduous than picking cotton, and the plantation quickly

TREASURES OUTSIDE THE CITY **153**

became known as "Hellhole on the Brazos." Many of the convicts—disproportionately African American men—died young.

After the practice of convict leasing was outlawed in 1912, the company-owned town of Sugar Land began attracting German and Czech workers from the Schulenberg-Flatonia area of the Texas Hill Country. The Imperial Mill, built in 1905, processed raw sugar brought in through the port of Galveston or by train from Louisiana.

By 1932, Imperial Sugar Company was the only remaining sugar manufacturer in Texas. The company struggled through the Great Depression. After an unsuccessful attempt to process figs, it was a loan from the Reconstruction Finance Corporation that kept the company afloat.

Things took a turn during World War II, when the Sugar Act lifted limits on imports, and the Imperial Sugar Company provided all sugar from Texas to Louisiana. In the 1990s, the company was the largest processor and refiner of sugar in the US.

While the sugar refinery shuttered in 2003, the corporate offices of Imperial Sugar remain in Sugar Land. The planned communities of First Colony and Sweetwater occupy the former sugarcane fields. The crown logo that adorns many bags of sugar also features on the Sugar Land city seal.

Sadly, prison farms continue to operate in Texas to this day. The Old Imperial Farm Cemetery on Easton Avenue just south of Hwy 90, serves as the final resting place for many of the prisoners who died while working the local sugar plantations after convict leasing was abolished in 1912. The Houston Museum of Natural Science at Sugar Land occupies the former prison barracks of the Central State Prison Farm.

1868
Oldest Funeral Home in Texas
J. Levy & Termini Funeral Home
2128 Broadway Ave. J, Galveston, TX

Joseph Levy, a French immigrant from the Alsace region and the eldest of nine siblings, moved from New York to Galveston in 1867, lured by the booming economy at the time. His brother Benjamin soon joined him, and the two founded what would become the oldest funeral home in Texas in 1868.

In the earliest years, J. Levy and Bro. wasn't actually a funeral home at all, but a company that bought and sold horses and mules. The brothers soon expanded to renting and selling carriages.

Funeral homes did not yet exist in those days. When someone passed, families were responsible for making all the necessary arrangements: hiring a carpenter to build a casket, arranging for a minister, and transporting the body by buggy or carriage to the burial place. Many families didn't have the financial means to own their own transportation, so they turned to the Levy brothers.

Recognizing the opportunity to provide a vital service to bereaved families in their time of need, the brothers again expanded their services by helping manage preparations for burial. The term "undertaker" comes from this act of undertaking funeral preparations on behalf of the family. They purchased a horse-drawn hearse for funeral transportation. By the end of the century, undertaking made up the bulk of business, with Ben appointed overseer of many of the burials following the 1900 hurricane that killed thousands of residents.

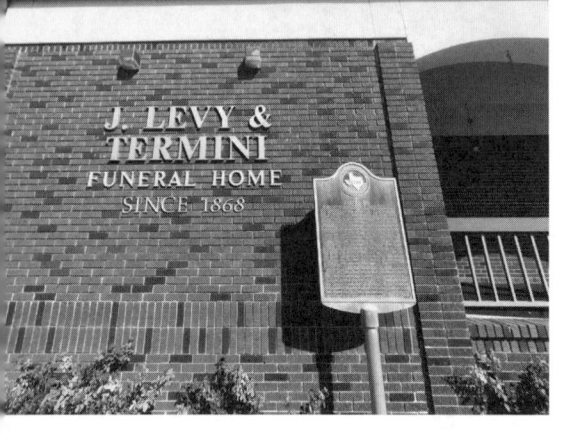

Change came again in 1908 when Ben Levy passed away, and his brother Joseph retired. Sam and Jack, the eldest sons of Joseph and Ben, respectively, took over their fathers' business, eliminating the horse trade element and adding an ambulance service. Horse-drawn hearses made way for the motorized versions in 1916, and, by 1926, after Jack sold his portion of the business, Sam was operating a full-service funeral home on the corner of Broadway and 22nd Street.

Native Galvestonians D. J. and Jill Russo Termini purchased the business in 2001, with a commitment to continue the century-and-a-half-long legacy of caring for Galveston families. D. J. himself is a second-generation funeral director.

Learn more about one of humankind's oldest cultural rituals at the National Museum of Funeral History, located just north of Houston. See the country's largest collection of funeral service items, including caskets, coffins, hearses, and mourning items from around the globe.

——————————————1890
Oldest Drugstor in Texas
Star Drug Store
510 23rd St., Galveston, TX

S tar Drug Store in Galveston is no stranger to historic superlatives. Besides being the oldest drugstore in Texas, it also was home to the first desegregated lunch counter in Galveston and boasts one of the oldest porcelain neon Coca-Cola signs still in existence today.

It all started in 1886, when the Scanlon family—known for their real estate ventures—hired Irish architect Nicholas Joseph Clayton to construct a pair of buildings downtown. These would become the Levy Building and the Star Drug Store, which opened for business in 1890. Clayton would go on to become one of Houston and Galveston's most notable architects, so much so that the period from 1870 to 1890 would become known as the "Clayton Era."

Throughout its more than a century of existence, the shop has changed ownership multiple times, survived a fire and three hurricanes (including the Storm of 1900), and witnessed its fair share of history.

With all those years come the inevitable whispers and stories that the Star may have some full-time residents of the spectral variety. Construction workers during renovations complained that their tools were moved around, and the men's bathroom sometimes locked with no one inside.

Star Drug Store operated exclusively as a pharmacy until a soda fountain was added in 1917. While the shop no longer fills prescriptions, you still can have a fountain soda or egg cream at the original horseshoe-shaped lunch counter, its façade embedded with red tile stars. These days, the Star serves all-American comfort food for breakfast and lunch. The original glass-fronted cabinets display nostalgic gifts and collectibles, rather than pills and tinctures.

The current owners rent out the loft space above the drugstore to visitors—a historic stay complete with a full kitchen, washer and dryer, and its own private entrance.

Star Drug Store occupies a historic building in downtown Galveston, just a couple of blocks from the centuries-old buildings of the Historic Strand District. To satisfy a sweet tooth, stop in to La King's Confectionery, an old-fashioned candy shop with its own 1920s soda fountain.

1904

OLDEST OIL FIELD
HUMBLE OIL FIELD
Humble, TX

Texas history took a turn on January 10, 1901, when petroleum engineer Anthony F. Lucas tapped a gusher in the Spindletop oil field that began producing an estimated 75,000 barrels of oil a day.

Spindletop was located on a salt dome about 85 miles east of Houston. Oil prospectors soon began searching the Texas coast for other places to drill. While local Humble resident James H. Slaughter had noticed oil bubbles in the San Jacinto River as early as 1887, the area northeast of Houston wasn't taken seriously as a drilling prospect until the oilmen came into town and "discovered" oil in 1904. By the end of 1905, two dozen wells were pumping "black gold" from the ground.

"Beatty No. 2 Gushes at Humble," the front page of the *Houston Chronicle* declared on January 9, 1905. Oilmen had found Houston's first major oil field. Property values skyrocketed in the town, and the population began to grow. By 1905, Humble was the biggest oil producer in Texas. The Humble Oil and Refining Co.—a predecessor of ExxonMobil—was founded here in 1911.

Another story was playing out in Houston proper that would have an equally big impact on Houston's trajectory. Developer Jesse Jones built a 10-story skyscraper with the express purpose of luring the Texas Company (now Texaco) out of Beaumont and

TREASURES OUTSIDE THE CITY **159**

"Humble oil fields" by Frank J. Schlueter (1916). Photo courtesy of the Museum of Houston and the Houston Metropolitan Research Center

into Houston. He did so by offering the building for just $2,000 per month—an offer Texas Company founder Joseph Cullinan couldn't pass up.

"Houston seems to me to be the coming center of the oil business," Cullinan wrote in a 1905 letter. His words couldn't have been more true.

Houston, with no deepwater harbor at the time, easily could have become the gateway to Beaumont. Instead, thanks to the Humble oil field, the opening of the Houston Ship Channel in 1914, and people like Jones and Cullinan, it became the "Energy Capital of the World."

All that you'll see of the oil field is a small historical marker on Farm to Market Rd. 1960 outside of Humble. The historic Humble Building on 1212 Main St. in downtown Houston once was the original headquarters of Humble Oil.

1904
OLDEST LIBRARY IN TEXAS
ROSENBERG LIBRARY
2310 Sealy Ave., Galveston, TX

Henry Rosenberg was born in Bilten, Switzerland, in 1824. He came to Galveston in 1843, where he worked as a clerk at a dry goods store. He went on to become one of the wealthiest men in Texas, making his fortune in banking, real estate, and transportation.

Rosenberg had no children, and when he died in 1893, he left more than $600,000 of his estate as an endowment for a public library. The Beaux Arts–style Rosenberg Library was dedicated on June 22, 1904 (Henry Rosenberg's birthday), making it the oldest continuously operating library in Texas. A year later, it absorbed the Galveston Public Library (formerly the Galveston Mercantile Library, from 1871) and became the official public library for the city of Galveston.

The library has amassed an extensive collection throughout its existence, well beyond the scope of a typical public library. It serves as the headquarters for the Galveston and Texas History Center, which collects photos, artifacts, and documents related to the city and early Texas history.

Highlights of the collection include Karankawa pottery shards, Sam Houston's dueling pistols, a pair of glass decanters taken from General Santa Anna's tent at the Battle of San Jacinto, a letter Sam Houston penned to President Andrew Jackson about the annexation of Texas, and gambling chips from the legendary Balinese Room.

When Hurricane Ike delivered a direct blow to Galveston in 2008, the entire first floor was submerged in 10 feet of murky water. The first floor of the library reopened in 2013 with a new state-of-the-art floodgate and windows made from hurricane-rated aquarium glass.

If you visit the annex building of Central High School, notice the words "Colored Branch of Rosenberg Library" carved above the west entrance. During segregation in the 20th century, this was the first public library for African Americans in the state. It operated from 1905 to 1958, when the main library finally opened to people of all races.

1907
Oldest Hatter
Shudde Bros. Hatters
1502 Farm to Market Rd. 1489, Brookshire, TX

Fans of old John Wayne classics like *The Alamo and Hellfighters* will not be strangers to Houston's oldest hatmaker. Shudde Bros. Hatters, founded in Houston in 1907, once customized cowboy hats for the actor to wear on filming locations just outside the city.

And the Duke wasn't the only famous customer. Shudde Bros. has made hats for everyone from Roy Rogers to the Mercury 7 astronauts to George Bush. Shudde Bros. served General Sam Houston posthumously by restoring one of his hats in 1936 for a museum display. The company even gifted a Stetson to John F. Kennedy after his visit to Houston in November 1963. He was presented the hat in Fort Worth, just hours before his assassination.

Photo courtesy of Shudde Bros. Hatters

The Shudde family moved from Carmine, Texas, to Houston in 1901. Al Shudde, then a teenager, got a job working for a German hatter in the area. When his boss decided to return to Europe, Al opened his own small shop, Shudde Southern Hat Company, on Trinity Avenue downtown. Al's brothers Ben, Walter, John, and Herbert soon joined the business, and, in 1914, the siblings opened a hat factory next door.

Photo courtesy of Shudde Bros. Hatters

During its precisely 100-year run in downtown, the business was passed to Al's son Weldon and Weldon's son Neal, who runs it today.

On June 30, 2007—a hundred years to the day from the company's founding—Neal moved Shudde Bros. Hatters to the Brookwood Community, 40 miles west of downtown Houston in the town of Brookshire. Brookwood, a nonprofit residential community, provides vocational programs for adults with disabilities.

In addition to traditional, steam-shaped felt cowboy hats, customers can purchase dress straw hats, top hats, derby hats, and even hats in the style of the Australian Outback or Indiana Jones. "The Western fashion is led by the rodeo circles," Neal wrote in *Texas Monthly*. "Some of the rodeo stars are changing the crowns a little bit, making them more boxy. The style of the brim changes gradually over the years, so you don't have the same look 20 years running."

All proceeds go toward supporting the community.

The town of Brookshire got its start as a thriving agricultural community producing melons, corn, pecans, and cotton in the mid-1800s. Learn more about the history of the region at the Waller County Historical Museum.

—1911
OLDEST SEAFOOD RESTAURANT IN TEXAS
Gaido's Seafood Restaurant
3828 Seawall Blvd., Galveston, TX

In 1911, the same year that air-conditioning was invented, Italian immigrant San Giacinto "Cinto" Gaido started serving fresh Gulf seafood to Galveston beachgoers from the former Murdoch's bathhouse on the 21st Street pier.

A giant blue crab perched on the roof welcomes diners to Gaido's Seafood Restaurant more than a century later. The current location at the Seawall and 39th Street first opened as a drive-in in 1936 before transitioning into a fine-dining establishment where Galveston locals would dress up for a night out.

It's now found itself somewhere in between casual and formal. Despite the waiters in starched shirts and bow ties and the pristine white tablecloths, Gaido's doesn't feel formal or stuffy. The walls of the dining room feature vintage photographs, antique diving helmets, and other artifacts that tell the story of Galveston through the past century.

(For the full upscale experience, make reservations at The Pelican Club in the back.)

Gulf seafood shines on the menu, with signature dishes like Watkins Bisque, a creamy seafood soup with baby shrimp and pureed vegetables, and cornmeal-fried oysters. The menu is always seasonal. During the summer months, when Gulf oysters are out of season, they're flown in from the East Coast.

In 2010, the Gaido family published a cookbook honoring the restaurant's 100-year history, entitled *Gaido's Famous Seafood Restaurant*. The book features some of the restaurant's most beloved recipes, like crustless pecan pie, Shrimp Peques (jalapeño and cheese-stuffed Gulf shrimp wrapped in bacon), and Cy's Demise grilled oysters.

Photo courtesy of Galveston Island Convention & Visitors Bureau

---

Gaido's sits just across Seawall Boulevard from the beach on a stretch of Gulf coast lined with seafood restaurants. It's a short walk to the Historic Pleasure Pier.

—————————1911
Oldest Barber Shop in Texas
Shepard's Barber Shop
116 Simonton St., Conroe, TX

In August 1955, a 21-year-old Elvis Presley took a seat in a barber chair at Shepard's Barber Shop for a haircut before taking the stage at Conroe High School—one of many performances in Houston that year. He paid $1.

Aside from claiming The King on its clientele list, this Conroe barber shop also ranks as the oldest continuously operating barber shop in Texas. More than a century's worth of memorabilia covers its walls, and more than a few customers have been coming here since they were kids; some of their parents and grandparents got *their* hair cut at Shepard's.

After a February 21, 1911, fire swept through downtown Conroe, destroying 65 wooden structures, Conroe began rebuilding under a new fire code that prohibited combustible buildings. Pete West and his son Jack constructed a two-story brick building known as the West Building. Next door, using the leftover bricks, Pete also built a smaller structure that would come to be called the Little Jack West Building.

This 1911 red brick structure has housed a barbershop continuously since 1912. Leon Apostolo—one of five barbers who owned the shop over the course of its history—started cutting hair at the shop when he was only 17. After four decades,

Apostolo went on to purchase the business from his boss, Bob Shepard, in 2013.

Stepping into Shepard's is a bit like stepping back in time. Prices have gone up a bit since Elvis's days, but not much else has changed. Customers still sit on green vinyl barber chairs. The hat stand, Coke machine, and checkerboard game in the waiting area also are vintage. And that's how Shepard's customers like it.

"In the fast-paced times we live in, they can come in here and feel like, wow, 'I remember this from when I was a kid,'" said Apostolo in a 2015 interview with *The Courier*. "It takes them to a simpler time when things were at a much slower pace."

For a historic haircut a bit closer to central Houston, take a seat at Doug's Barber Shop in the Heights. There's been a barber shop in this space since it was built in 1929.

1916
OLDEST TEX-MEX RESTAURANT IN TEXAS
THE ORIGINAL MEXICAN CAFE
1401 Market St., Galveston, TX

The Original Mexican Cafe has been serving Tex-Mex food from the same location on Galveston Island since it first opened in 1916. It's now believed to be the oldest continuously running Tex-Mex restaurant in the state, predating El Fenix in Dallas by two years.

The colorful restaurant occupies a former corner store on the corner of 14th and Market Streets in the East End Historic District. Ramon and Hattie Guzman opened the restaurant and lived upstairs. Ramon, born in Mexico in 1883, came to the United States in 1903 and married in 1913. Hattie owned the restaurant until her death in 1951.

While The Original Mexican Cafe has changed ownership a few times since, it's always been family owned and has always stuck to its Tex-Mex roots. The menu features a lineup of Tex-Mex classics—enchiladas, tacos al carbon, quesadillas, combination plates, and tamales topped with chili con carne—alongside more traditional Mexican specialties like menudo. The chile con queso and mole enchiladas also win rave reviews.

—1922

Oldest Butcher
Stanton Meats
219 N. Taylor St., Alvin, TX

E. J. and Leah Ann Stanton moved from their home in Wisconsin to Alvin, Texas with their two children, Mildred and George, in 1909. The family began raising cattle on land north of town. In 1922, they decided to open a feed store and cleverly chose a location across from the town's ice house, figuring they'd drum up business from customers passing by to get their ice.

George began helping his father buy, raise, and sell cattle. As a teenager, he'd worked as a laborer in Kansas and Oklahoma during the wheat harvest so he could send money home to buy more cattle. Shortly after his father's death in 1929, George expanded the feed store's offerings to include a hardware store, pharmacy, and meat market.

Photo courtesy of Stanton Meats

It was believed at the time that the humid climate of the Texas Gulf Coast was unsuitable for raising cattle. George soon proved this wrong when he began selling quality beef he raised himself. His Hereford steers were so good that they took home the Grand Champion prize at the Houston Fat Stock Show (now the Houston Livestock Show & Rodeo) twice, once in 1934 and again in 1947.

Allen Stanton, George's grandson, now runs the family business. Stanton's Shopping Center in downtown Alvin comprises a grocery store and meat market, hardware store, feed store, and propane pumping station. Besides quality beef, Stanton Meats is known for its South Texas Smoked Beef Sticks, fajita meat, and exotic meat sausages made from kangaroo, alligator, buffalo, or wild boar, among others.

The town of Alvin, located between Houston and the Texas Gulf Coast, dates to 1845. Stop by the Alvin Historical Museum to learn more about the area's history, visit the Historical Train Depot (once part of the Santa Fe Rail Line), or find a piece of history to take home at the sprawling Alvin Antique Center.

Photo courtesy of Stanton Meats

SOURCES

Oldest Tree: www.chron.com/culture/article/houston-hanging-tree-downtown-history-debunked-16374370.php; www.nwf.org/Educational-Resources/Wildlife-Guide/Plants-and-Fungi/Southern-Live-Oak; www.epperts.com/lfa/BB80.html.

Oldest Port: buffalobayou.org/visit/destination/allens-landing; www.chron.com/entertainment/article/Peering-into-Allen-s-Landing-s-murky-history-1548884.php; texashistory.unt.edu/ark:/67531/metapth47882/m1/3.

Oldest Religious Congregation: www.christchurchcathedral.org; www.houstonchronicle.com/news/houston-texas/houston/article/Christ-Church-Cathedral-s-story-parallels-5321127.php; www.tshaonline.org/handbook/entries/protestant-episcopal-church.

Oldest Building: www.heritagesociety.org/kellum-noble-house; www.houstonchronicle.com/life/home/design/article/Kellum-Noble-House-reopens-in-Sam-Houston-Park-14864801.php; houstonhistorymagazine.org/wp-content/uploads/2020/06/Kellum-Noble-House.pdf.

Oldest Commercial Building: easttexashistory.org/items/show/140; www.thc.state.tx.us/public/upload/NR%20TX%20inventory%202-7-12.pdf; atlas.thc.state.tx.us/NR/pdfs/79002963/79002963.pdf; www.houstonpress.com/restaurants/best-of-houston-2021-best-burger-11716855; savingplaces.org/stories/la-carafe-in-houston-texas#.YTjADVNKj6g; texashighways.com/eat-drink/return-to-la-carafe-houston; www.thehoustonians.com/articles/have-a-blast-with-the-past-at-la-carafe; www.houstonchronicle.com/culture/main/article/Life-size-painting-gets-a-face-lift-and-returns-5347995.php.

Oldest Law Firm: www.tshaonline.org/handbook/entries/baker-botts; www.tshaonline.org/handbook/entries/gray-peter-w; www.tshaonline.org/handbook/entries/baker-james-addison-jr; www.bakerbotts.com; www.houstonchronicle.com/business/article/Houston-s-Baker-Botts-marks-its-175th-anniversary-6627976.php#photo-8917894.

Oldest Catholic Church: www.annunciationcc.org; www.tshaonline.org/handbook/entries/church-of-the-annunciation-houston; www.foxnews.com/us/faithful-houston-astros-fans-flocking-to-buy-team-themed-rosary-beads.

Oldest Catholic School: www.tshaonline.org/handbook/entries/incarnate-word-academy; www.incarnateword.org/about/our-history.

Oldest Hospital: www.tmc.edu/about-tmc; www.sjmctx.org/about-us; www.chron.com/local/history/medical-science/article/Bishop-Byrne-Dedicates-St-Joseph-Annex-10611853.php; www.chron.com/news/health/article/Historic-St-Joseph-hospital-facing-uncertain-fate-1920020.php.

Oldest Performing Arts Organization: houstonsymphony.org/wp-content/uploads/2021/09/History-of-the-Houston-Symphony_21-22_FINAL.pdf; www.tshaonline.org/handbook/entries/houston-symphony-orchestra; www.dallasnews.com/arts-entertainment/architecture/2015/05/23/the-houston-symphony-proud-history-problematic-home; www.visithoustontexas.com/theater/venues/jones-hall/

Oldest Hotel: www.visithoustontexas.com/hotels/unique-and-historic-hotels; www.historichotels.org/us/hotels-resorts/the-sam-houston-hotel/history.php; atlas.thc.state.tx.us/NR/pdfs/02000276/02000276.pdf.

Oldest Skyscraper: www.texasce.org/tce-news/start-of-the-houston-skyline-neils-esperson-building; cameronmanagement.com/wp-content/uploads/2018/08/A-Glimpse-in-Time-The-Magnificent-Espersons-06.06.18.pdf; www.houstonchronicle.com/news/houston-texas/bayou-city-history/article/Birth-of-a-skyline-Niels-Esperson-Building-10966126.php#photo-5046941; abc13.com/esperson-building-for-sale/2163290/

Oldest Theater Company: www.tshaonline.org/handbook/entries/alley-theatre; www.alleytheatre.org/about-us; www.houstontx.gov/planning/HistoricPres/landmarks/14PL120_Alley_Theatre_FINAL.pdf.

Oldest Permanent Opera Company: www.tshaonline.org/handbook/entries/houston-grand-opera; www.houstongrandopera.org/about-us.

Oldest Chinese Restaurant: abc13.com/china-garden-founder-death-marian-mamma-jue-asiatown-restaurant-historic-houston/10357429; www.chron.com/news/houston-texas/houston/article/China-Garden-oldest-Chinese-restaurant-in-Houston-12625341.php; houston.culturemap.com/news/restaurants-bars/10-23-12-12-01-the-american-dream-lives-on-at-houstons-oldest-and-some-say-best-chinese-restaurant/#slide=0; www.originalchinagardenhouston.com; www.dignitymemorial.com/obituaries/houston-tx/marian-jue-10065595.

Oldest Martin Luther King Day Parade in the United States: originalmlkparade.org/about; apnews.com/article/c39743ca881b47c9b10cacc6ca40926c; www.houstonpress.com/arts/why-does-houston-have-two-mlk-parades-10075236; kinginstitute.stanford.edu/encyclopedia/drum-major-instinct.

Oldest Art Car Parade in the World: www.thehoustonartcarparade.com/history-of-the-houston-art-car-para; www.orangeshow.org/orange-show-history

Oldest Cemetery: www.houstontx.gov/parks/founderscemetery.html; www.dar.org/national-society/historic-sites-and-properties/founders-memorial-park-cemetery-old-city-cemetery; www.tshaonline.org/handbook/entries/founders-memorial-cemetery; www.tshaonline.org/handbook/entries/collinsworth-james; www.visithoustontexas.com/about-houston/history; www.pgal.com/projects/city-of-houston-bethel-park.

Oldest Black Neighborhood: www.click2houston.com/houston-life/2020/02/04/houston-history-the-citys-oldest-and-most-important-black-neighborhood/; houston.culturemap.com/news/city-life/01-21-15-freedmens-town-historic-brick-roads-get-a-last-minute-reprieve-as-judge-temporarily-backs-preservationists; houstonhistorymagazine.org/wp-content/uploads/2011/04/meeks-freedmans-town.pdf; www.tshaonline.org/handbook/entries/fourth-ward-houston; www.tshaonline.org/handbook/entries/freedmens-settlements; houstonfreedmenstown.org; www.houstonchronicle.com/politics/houston/article/Houston-City-Council-votes-to-make-Freedmen-s-16252129.php; www.blackpast.org/african-american-history/fourth-ward-houston-texas-1839.

Oldest Professionally Designed Cemetery: wanderwisdom.com/travel-destinations/Glenwood-Cemetery-Houston-Whos-Who-of-Spectacular-Grave-Sites; historichouston1836.com/glenwood-cemetery; af-legacy-prd.americanforests.org/magazine/article/in-the-garden-cemetery-the-revival-of-americas-first-urban-parks/; www.glenwoodcemetery.org; www.tshaonline.org/handbook/entries/glenwood-cemetery; www.houstonchronicle.com/lifestyle/home-design/article/The-River-Oaks-of-cemeteries-See-the-stunning-16335281.php.

Oldest African American Cemetery: www.tshaonline.org/handbook/entries/olivewood-cemetery; web.archive.org/web/20070415070243/www.houstontx.gov/

hr/savvypages/archives/fall05/fall05_cemetery.htm; www.descendantsofolivewood. org/about-olivewood; www.houstonchronicle.com/local/gray-matters/article/ Sign-Language-At-Olivewood-Cemetery-living-6083894.php#photo-1514899; www. click2houston.com/houston-life/2021/02/05/keeping-the-history-at-houstons-olivewood-cemetery-alive; texashistoricalmarkers.weebly.com/olivewood-cemetery.html.

Oldest Intact Neighborhood: www.houstontx.gov/planning/HistoricPres/HistoricPreservationManual/historic_districts/old_sixth_ward.html; www.thc.texas.gov/public/upload/preserve/survey/highway/Old%20Sixth%20Ward%20Historic%20District%20Houston.pdf; houstonhistorymagazine.org/wp-content/uploads/2011/07/Sixth-Ward.pdf; www.neighborhoods.com/blog/your-guide-to-the-six-wards-of-houston; offcite.rice.edu/2011/11/Cite_87_Old_Sixth_Ward_Historic_District_Zepeda.pdf.

Oldest Boot Maker: tylerpaper.com/news/business/old-houston-boot-business-maidas-where-boots-start-at-2-000-and-last-for-years/article_7bbacd33-ed6f-54bd-b26a-9c6c24893e31.html; www.maidas.com.

Oldest Suburb: medium.com/save-texas-history/mapping-houston-heights-houstons-first-suburb-14b46390686b; www.tshaonline.org/handbook/entries/houston-heights-tx; www.houstonpress.com/arts/the-changing-face-of-houston-the-heights-then-and-now-6383904?storyPage=3; houstonheights.org/contact.

Oldest Firehouse: www.houstontx.gov/planning/HistoricPres/landmarks/97L041_Fire-Station_No7_Houston-Fire-Museum_2403_Milam.pdf; www.houstonfiremuseum.org; catalog.archives.gov/OpaAPI/media/40972254/content/electronic-records/rg-079/NPS_TX/86000798.pdf; www.firehero.org/2021/04/26/memorial-monday-texas-city-disaster.

Oldest Brick-Paved Street: www.old6ward.org/our-homes/land-people; www.historicpavement.com/vitrified-brick-overview; www.thc.texas.gov/public/upload/preserve/survey/highway/Old%20Sixth%20Ward%20Historic%20District%20Houston.pdf; www.tshaonline.org/handbook/entries/sixth-ward-houston; www.chron.com/news/houston-texas/houston/article/freedmen-s-town-bricks-houston-installation-paused-11114702.php.

Oldest University: www.jstor.org/stable/2963155; www.rice.edu/about; www.tshaonline.org/handbook/entries/rice-william-marsh; www.tshaonline.org/handbook/entries/rice-university; news.rice.edu/2020/11/09/the-legal-battle-over-desegregating-rice-gives-context-to-historic-decision.

Oldest Local Fast-Food Chain: jamesconeyisland.com/about-us; www.bizjournals.com/houston/morning_call/2013/11/after-90-years-james-coney-island.html; www.houstoniamag.com/news-and-city-life/2013/07/dogs-of-yore-july-2013.

Oldest Outdoor Theater: www.milleroutdoortheatre.com/past-and-present; www.tshaonline.org/handbook/entries/miller-outdoor-theatre; houstonhistorymagazine.org/wp-content/uploads/2011/01/Harwell-Miller-Outdoor-Theatre.pdf.

Oldest Museum: www.visithoustontexas.com/listings/museum-of-fine-arts-houston/19535; www.tshaonline.org/handbook/entries/museum-of-fine-arts-houston; www.mfah.org/press/mfah-to-open-steven-holl-designed-nancy-rich-kinder-building-november-1-2020; houmuse.org/meet-the-museums-of-zone-3.

Oldest Statue: www.houstontx.gov/parks/artinparks/samhoustonmonument.html; www.shsu.edu/today@sam/samhouston/HouGia.html; houstonhistorymagazine.org/wp-content/uploads/2013/07/Teich-final-proof.pdf.

Oldest Underground Reservoir: buffalobayou.org/visit/destination/the-cistern; www.houstonchronicle.com/life/gray/article/Gray-Buffalo-Bayou-s-dark-secret-2736594.php.

Oldest Public Garden: www.mfah.org/visit/bayou-bend-collection-and-gardens/bayou-bend-gardens; www.tshaonline.org/handbook/entries/hogg-ima; www.tshaonline.org/handbook/entries/bayou-bend.

Oldest Ice House: punchdrink.com/articles/inside-west-alabama-ice-house-history-daniel-krieger-bar-tripping-houston; explorepartsunknown.com/houston/a-love-letter-to-houstons-west-alabama-ice-house; www.nytimes.com/1998/08/23/us/icehouses-in-texas-vanishing-like-their-frosty-beer-on-a-warm-afternoon.html; www.npr.org/2006/06/29/5522825/texas-icehouses-melt-away; www.chron.com/entertainment/article/Cover-story-Regulars-at-West-Alabama-Icehouse-2113141.php; www.texasmonthly.com/being-texan/texas-primer-the-icehouse; solutions.rdtonline.com/blog/a-brief-history-of-the-texas-ice-house; www.houstonchronicle.com/local/gray-matters/article/What-icehouses-mean-to-Houston-7044752.php; twitter.com/icehousehouston; texashighways.com/eat-drink/the-ice-age-houston-icehouses; www.visithoustontexas.com/listings/west-alabama-ice-house/20653.

Oldest Fish Market: www.airlineseafood.net; www.papercitymag.com/restaurants/airline-seafood-houston-restaurant-scene-chefs-chris-shepherd; www.houstoniamag.com/news-and-city-life/2016/03/catch-of-the-day-houstons-7-best-seafood-markets-march-2016.

Oldest Bakery: abc13.com/houston-bakery-baking-a-cake-food-moellers/7805512; moellersbakery.com.

Oldest BBQ Joint: www.houstonpress.com/restaurants/a-smoked-out-tradition-pizzitolas-bar-b-cue-11453496; www.houstonchronicle.com/food-culture/restaurants-bars/bbq/article/A-new-era-begins-at-Pizzitola-s-Bar-B-Cue-16003526.php; pizzitolasbbq.com/history; www.houstonchronicle.com/entertainment/restaurants-bars/bbq/article/Know-your-regional-styles-of-barbecue-8122411.php.

Oldest Hardware Store: www.chron.com/business/article/Family-owned-hardware-store-defies-the-odds-1702743.php; www.southlandhardware.com/tool-hardware-sales; www.houstonchronicle.com/local/gray-matters/article/Sign-Language-The-Almost-Everything-Store-6058931.php.

Oldest Doughnut Shop: myshipleydonuts.com/about-us/shipley-history; abc13.com/shipley-do-nuts-history-of-donuts-in-houston-the-great-depression/2669984; abc13.com/society/local-artist-unveils-first-shipleys-mural-in-houston/4699679; www.shipleydonutsdash.com.

Oldest Cafeteria: cleburnecafeteria.com/history; www.papercitymag.com/restaurants/cleburne-cafeteria-houston-owner-george-mickelis-endures-lubsy-closing; davewardshouston.com/cleburne-cafeteria-houston; www.foodandwine.com/travel/restaurants/best-cafeterias-america; houstonfoodfinder.com/foodfinds/houston-comfort-food-classic-evolves-for-2020-diners; www.britannica.com/topic/cafeteria.

Oldest Fountain: www.chron.com/neighborhood/heights/news/article/Hyde-Park-group-dives-into-fountain-project-4802453.php; hydeparkhouston.org/wp-content/uploads/Lamar-Park-Brochure-Dolphin-Fountain.August2014.pdf; houstonparksboard.org/donate?search=dolphin.

Oldest Bar: leonslounge.com; www.chron.com/culture/main/article/New-life-on-the-horizon-for-Houston-s-oldest-bar-6424715.php; www.facebook.com/LeonsLounge.Est.1947.

Oldest Deli: www.nielsensdelicatessen.com; my-table.com/getting-nosy-with-richard-andersen-of-nielsens; www.houstonpress.com/best-of/2002/food-and-drink/best-deli-6604466; www.tagsaletastes.com/2015/06/25/retro-dining-nielsens-delicatessen.

Oldest Gay Organization: thedianafoundation.org/page/history-of-the-diana-foundation; www.outsmartmagazine.com/2010/03/the-dianas-part-one; www.houstonlgbthistory.org/banner1954.html; Interview with president, September 29, 2021.

Oldest Tobacconist: communityimpact.com/news/2019/07/09/the-briar-shoppe-rice-village; www.briarshoppecigars.com.

Oldest Stadium: www.nrgpark.com/nrg-park-facilities-2/nrg-astrodome; www.ballparksofbaseball.com/ballparks/astrodome; savingplaces.org/places/the-astrodome#.YRpovFNKj6g; www.tshaonline.org/handbook/entries/astrodome; www.thc.texas.gov/public/upload/preserve/national_register/final/Astrodome%20NR.pdf; www.newspapers.com/image/?clipping_id=35848964&fcfToken=eyJhbGciOiJIUzI1NiIsInR5cCI6IkpXVCJ9.eyJmcmVlLXZpZXctaWQiOjM4MjE4ODEzMiwiaWF0IjoxNjI5MTIyMzMyLCJleHAiOjE2MjkyMDg3MzJ9.pW9UkDtgQN3ug49gJh-TDokoCtdQ7gfD8DiC0jx0W7A.

Oldest Sports Bar: www.visithoustontexas.com/listings/griffs-irish-pub/20629; www.griffsirishpub.com; houston.culturemap.com/news/city-life/03-15-14-irish-beauty-ast-patricks-day-queen-is-crowned-at-houstons-most-unique-irish-bar/#slide=0.

Oldest Italian Restaurant: www.mikericcetti.com/blog/a-passegiata-through-houstons-italian-restaurant-history; abc13.com/tonys-tony-vallone-trump-met-nixon-houston-fine-dining/6074602; www.texasmonthly.com/food/tony-vallone-houston-restaurateur-dies-tonys; www.chron.com/local/history/culture-scene/article/Tony-s-restaurant-played-heady-role-in-Houston-s-8324057.php; www.houstonchronicle.com/life/article/Tony-s-celebrates-five-decades-6177971.php; www.tonyshouston.com.

Oldest Hindu Temple: iskconhouston.org; iskconofhouston.wordpress.com/history; www.intechopen.com/chapters/68484; centers.iskcondesiretree.com/united-states-of-america; www.thehindu.com/society/faith/govinda-explained/article25692498.ece; www.britannica.com/topic/Hare-Krishna; iskconnews.org/grand-new-houston-temple-to-finally-open-this-may.

Oldest Bookstore: www.brazosbookstore.com; www.chron.com/news/houston-texas/article/Group-saves-Brazos-Bookstore-from-closure-1902066.php; www.houstonchronicle.com/life/article/Brazos-Bookstore-Inprint-founder-Karl-Kilian-15791941.php; www.texasmonthly.com/arts-entertainment/remembering-karl-kilian-founder-of-houstons-brazos-bookstore.

Oldest Comic Shop: abc7.com/third-planet-sci-fi-superstore-tj-johnson-comic-books-houston-collectibles/6371385; www.houstoniamag.com/arts-and-culture/2020/09/third-planet-scifi-fantasy-superstor-45th-anniversary; www.houstonchronicle.com/news/houston-texas/houston/article/Comic-store-Third-Planet-alleges-Houston-hotel-16285087.php#photo-21184251; feldman.law/news/iconic-houston-comic-store-third-planet-files-lawsuit-using-full-color-comic-book.

Oldest Crawfish Restaurant: www.houstoniamag.com/eat-and-drink/houston-louisiana-crawfish-tradition; ragin-cajun.com/about; ragin-cajun.com/crawfish-season-is-here-2.

Oldest Vietnamese Restaurant: maishouston.com; www.houstonchronicle.com/entertainment/restaurants-bars/article/Anthony-Bourdain-s-history-with-Houston-12978378.php; www.tshaonline.org/handbook/entries/vietnamese; www.houstonpublicmedia.org/articles/news/2018/11/28/313247/decades-after-clashing-with-the-klan-a-thriving-vietnamese-community-in-texas.

Oldest African American Church: www.txcumc.org/newsdetail/oldest-churches-in-houston-separated-by-slavery-join-together-for-worship-for-special-service-13262431; thetumc.com/trinityprep; www.trinityeastumc.org/about-trinity-east; texasindependencetrail.com/plan-your-adventure/historic-sites-and-cities/sites/trinity-united-methodist-church; www.txcumc.org/newsdetail/oldest-churches-in-houston-separated-by-slavery-join-together-for-worship-for-special-service-13262431; www.waymarking.com/waymarks/WMY2VZ_Trinity_United_Methodist_Church; www.descendantsofolivewood.org/about-olivewood; www.hmdb.org/m.asp?m=171242.

Oldest Park: en.wikipedia.org/wiki/Emancipation_Park_(Houston); www.chron.com/opinion/editorials/article/Emancipation-Park-A-special-place-2236148.php; www.texasmonthly.com/the-culture/green-acres-2; houstonhistorymagazine.org/2012/07/emancipation-is-a-park-2; www.tshaonline.org/handbook/entries/juneteenth; www.houstonchronicle.com/projects/2021/juneteenth-emancipation-trail; www.ntma.com/houstons-emancipation-park-immortalizes-story-of-freedom.

Oldest 18-Hole Golf Course: www.houstontx.gov/municipalgolf/wortham/worthamrestoration.pdf; www.houstoniamag.com/travel-and-outdoors/2021/04/gus-wortham-park-golf-course-restoration-legacy; www.golfdigest.com/story/houstons-complete-revitalization-of-gus-wortham-municipal-course-is-a-model-for-other-cities-to-follow; www.guswortham.org; worthamparkfriends.wordpress.com/about-2-2/reni.

Oldest Recording Studio: www.sugarhillstudios713.com; www.tshaonline.org/handbook/entries/sugarhill-recording-studios; houston.culturemap.com/news/entertainment/01-22-10-the-sweet-sounds-of-sugar-hill-recording-studio; www.amazon.com/House-Hits-Houstons-SugarHill-Recording/dp/0292763182.

Oldest Soul Food Restaurant: houstonthisisit.com/about; houston.eater.com/maps/houston-classic-oldest-restaurants; www.youtube.com/watch?v=J0hdXxsz9nk.

Oldest Fajita Restaurant: www.tshaonline.org/handbook/entries/laurenzo-maria-ninfa-rodriguez; www.austinchronicle.com/food/2005-03-04/261130; www.gazettetimes.com/news/local/history-of-fajitas-is-short-flavor-is-not/article_2bc50150-5d0a-11e1-b076-0019bb2963f4.html.

Oldest Craft Brewery: www.saintarnold.com/about-us; www.downtownhouston.org/news/article/gospel-saint-arnold-texas-oldest-craft-brewery-houstons-newest-beer-garden-restaurant; www.khou.com/article/news/25-years-of-craft-beer-in-houston/285-7da58f38-7136-443a-9517-02b7adf3de8f; www.chron.com/business/article/Houstons-Saint-Arnold-Brewery-turns-22-years-old-7970364.php#taboola-11.

Oldest Jewish Congregation in Texas: www.beth-israel.org/about-us; texasalmanac.com/topics/culture/jewish/jewish-texans; www.tshaonline.org/handbook/entries/congregation-beth-israel-houston; atlas.thc.state.tx.us/Details/5507014339; blog.chron.com/bayoucityhistory/2011/02/congregation-beth-israel-through-the-years.

Oldest Haberdashery: www.waymarking.com/waymarks/WMZRW1_Hamilton_Shirts; hamiltonshirts.com/our-story; www.chron.com/local/history/economy-business/article/Hamilton-family-selling-shirts-here-for-over-100-12445686.php#photo-14733795; www.houstonchronicle.com/business/article/Hamilton-Shirts-well-suited-to-changing-tastes-13792494.php; hamiltonshirts.com/2018/07/31/houston-business-journal-sits-kelly-hamilton.

Oldest Women's Club: www.thewomansclubofhouston.org; en.wikipedia.org/wiki/Woman%27s_club_movement_in_the_United_States; www.womenshistory.org/articles/womens-clubs.

Oldest Independent, Nonparochial School: www.tshaonline.org/handbook/entries/kinkaid-school; www.kinkaid.org/explore/leadership/campus-history; www.usnews.com/education/k12/texas/the-kinkaid-school-327950.

Oldest Country Club: ricehistorycorner.com/2020/12/04/a-few-timely-comments-from-mr-wm-m-rice-1938; www.golfpass.com/travel-advisor/articles/old-texas-country-clubs; www.golftexas.com/golf-courses/south-east/houston/houston-country.htm; houston.culturemap.com/guide/entertainment/houston-country-club.

Oldest Restaurant: www.christies-restaurant.com; www.chron.com/news/houston-texas/houston/article/Christie-s-restaurant-says-goodbye-to-Bush-41-a-13437702.php; www.bizjournals.com/houston/news/2013/12/02/owner-of-popular-popular-houston.html.

Oldest Burger Joint: www.tshaonline.org/handbook/entries/princes-hamburgers; houston.eater.com/2020/10/1/21497092/houston-princes-hamburgers-reopening-sharpstown-park-golf-course; preview.houstonchronicle.com/dining/burger-friday-prince-s-hamburgers-at-15776236; www.foodservicenews.net/article-archive/culinary-curiosities-back-when-carhops-were-the-only-delivery-service/article_aba5a763-b340-52b7-91b2-caa2ea0a4737.html.

Oldest Tex-Mex Restaurant: www.molinascantina.com/about-history; www.houstonchronicle.com/food/article/Molina-s-Tex-Mex-restaurants-mark-75-years-in-9204023.php; www.houstonpress.com/restaurants/temples-of-tex-mex-a-diners-guide-to-the-states-oldest-mexican-restaurants-6573697.

Oldest Pizza Parlor: www.mikericcetti.com/blog/a-passegiata-through-houstons-italian-restaurant-history; www.antonios.com/history; www.chron.com/local/gray-matters/article/They-don-t-make-signs-like-that-anymore-5756245.php#photo-6868880.

Oldest Indian Restaurant: rajasweets.com; abc13.com/mahatma-gandhi-district-southwest-houston-indian-americans-india/10221736; abc13.com/localish/raja-sweets-is-texas-oldest-indian-restaurant/10223553.

Oldest Commercial Airport: www.houston.org/houston-data/monthly-update-aviation; www.tshaonline.org/handbook/entries/william-p-hobby-airport; www.chron.com/business/article/Houston-Hobby-Airport-celebrates-90th-birthday-11232715.php; www.fly2houston.com/newsroom/articles/hobby-airport-celebrates-90-years; www.fly2houston.com/newsroom/articles/george-bush-intercontinental-airport-ranks-best-us-airport-second-best-north-america-world-airport-a; www.fly2houston.com/hou/harmony-in-the-air; easttexashistory.org/items/show/144.

Oldest Urban Expressway: www.chron.com/news/houston-texas/transportation/article/Houston-Gulf-Freeway-turns-65-11723798.php; houstonhistorymagazine.org/wp-content/uploads/2011/11/V5-N2-McKinney-Gulf-Freeway.pdf.

Oldest Muslim Community: masjidwdmohammed.com; www.khou.com/article/news/more-mosques-being-built-in-houston-area/285-341987661; www.chron.com/life/houston-belief/article/U-S-sees-rise-of-Islamic-centers-3392670.php.

Oldest Continuously Operating Opera Company: gilbertandsullivan.org/history; www.eno.org/discover-opera/beginners-guide-gilbert-sullivan; www.chron.com/entertainment/music/article/Opera-For-love-of-operetta-2025189.php.

Oldest Public Television Station: www.pbs.org/spacestation/production/kuht.htm; www.houstonpublicmedia.org/about; houstonhistorymagazine.org/wp-content/uploads/2013/03/KUHT.pdf.

Oldest Kolache Shop: www.originalkolache.com/about-us; www.houstonchronicle.com/entertainment/restaurants-bars/reviews/article/Review-New-life-for-East-End-institution-11063950.php#photo-12700740; houston.eater.com/2015/1/28/7930073/a-tuesday-morning-breakfast-at-the-original-kolache-shoppe; www.highdrive.tv/businessmakers/kevin-dowd-original-kolache-shoppe; www.texascooppower.com/food/taste-of-texas/the-kolach-trail.

Oldest Buddhist Temple: www.hbvihara.org; hadistrict.org/2021/07/sri-lankan-buddhist-temple-preserves-quiet-and-calm-near-airport; oxfordre.com/americanhistory/view/10.1093/acrefore/9780199329175.001.0001/acrefore-9780199329175-e-320; www.bbc.co.uk/religion/religions/buddhism/subdivisions/theravada_1.shtml; tricycle.org/beginners/buddhism/buddhism-comes-to-america.

Oldest Operating Ferry: www.hctra.org/LynchburgFerry; www.tshaonline.org/handbook/entries/lynchs-ferry; www.chron.com/neighborhood/pasadena-news/article/Lynchburg-Ferry-carries-history-along-for-the-ride-2109535.php.

Oldest Town in Harris County: historicalcommission.harriscountytx.gov/Pages/Harrisburg.aspx; www.tshaonline.org/handbook/entries/harrisburg-tx-harris-county; www.tshaonline.org/handbook/entries/harris-county; www.chron.com/culture/main/article/Join-me-for-a-tour-of-an-East-End-gem-with-an-15650231.php.

Oldest Newspaper in Texas: www.galvnews.com; www.tshaonline.org/handbook/entries/galveston-news; web.archive.org/web/20050320192132/galvestondailynews.com/history.lasso?WCD=firsts.html; web.archive.org/web/20050320190709/galvestondailynews.com/history.lasso?WCD=didyouknow.html; www.galvnews.com/news/specialreports/free/article_e67ee2cd-4f52-5c17-a75e-8d04cfd342b5.html; texashistory.unt.edu/explore/collections/GVWN.

Oldest Business in Texas: www.tshaonline.org/handbook/entries/imperial-sugar-company; www.imperialsugarland.com/history; www.imperialsugarcompany.com/history; www.sugarlandtx.gov/1585/Imperial-Sugar-Mill; digitalprojects.rice.edu/wrc/convict-leasing/exhibits/show/sugarlandconvictleasing/history-of-convict-leasing; theclio.com/entry/76560; www.texasmonthly.com/articles/sugar-land-slave-convict-labor-history.

Oldest Funeral Home in Texas: www.jlevyfuneralhome.com/history; www.imortuary.com/funeral-homes/texas/galveston/j-levy-termini-funeral-home; www.funeralwise.com/learn/industry; www.galveston.com/whattodo/tours/self-guided-tours/historical-markers/j-levy-bro.

Oldest Drugstore in Texas: www.chron.com/this-forgotten-day-in-houston/article/Star-Drug-Reopens-in-Galveston-6250984.php; galvestonstardrug.com; vimeo.com/421285518; voyagehouston.com/interview/meet-natili-monsrud-star-drug-store-galveston-island; www.tshaonline.org/handbook/entries/clayton-nicholas-joseph.

Oldest Oil Field: www.texasmonthly.com/news-politics/evolution-energy-capital-world/#comments; corporate.exxonmobil.com/About-us/Who-we-are/Our-history; www.tshaonline.org/handbook/entries/oil-and-gas-industry; www.houstonpublicmedia.org/articles/news/2017/10/26/244823/the-boom-and-bust-of-moonshine-hill; www.wpowerproducts.com/news/why-did-houston-become-energy-capital-of-the-world; www.tshaonline.org/handbook/entries/texaco; www.tshaonline.org/handbook/entries/jones-jesse-holman; www.tshaonline.org/handbook/entries/cullinan-joseph-stephen; www.chron.com/local/history/economy-business/article/DRILL-STILL-GOING-DOWN-11155834.php#photo-12925934.

Oldest Library in Texas: www.houstonchronicle.com/life/article/New-page-in-Rosenberg-Library-history-4662162.php#photo-4908081; rosenberg-library.org/about/about-the-library/library-history-video; www.texasstandard.org/stories/why-three-libraries-claim-to-be-the-oldest-in-texas; www.tshaonline.org/handbook/entries/rosenberg-henry; www.tshaonline.org/handbook/entries/rosenberg-library.

Oldest Hatter: www.shudde.com/sound/weldon.wav; grapevinesource.com/2018/05/28/hats-off-to-houstons-historic-shudde-hats-local-family-has-made-hats-for-112-years; www.texasmonthly.com/the-culture/neal-shudde-hatter; www.tshaonline.org/handbook/entries/brookshire-tx.

SOURCES **179**

Oldest Seafood Restaurant in Texas: www.gaidos.com/about; texashighways.com/eat-drink/a-century-of-seafood-gaidos-galveston; www.houstonpress.com/best-of/2006/food-and-drink/best-seafood-restaurant-6605778; www.hmdb.org/m.asp?m=180028; www.chron.com/neighborhood/article/Gaido-s-Seafood-Restaurant-commemorates-100-9462833.php.

Oldest Barber Shop in Texas: abc13.com/htx-conroe-leon-apostolo-shepards-barber-shop/5470958; www.yourconroenews.com/neighborhood/moco/news/article/Historic-building-has-served-as-a-barber-shop-for-9501627.php; www.atlasobscura.com/places/shepards-barber-shop; www.yourconroenews.com/neighborhood/moco/news/article/Century-old-barbershop-reopens-to-loyal-customers-15259431.php; www.houstonchronicle.com/neighborhood/woodlands/news/article/Marking-history-at-Conroe-barbershop-of-9-decades-5946019.php.

Oldest Tex-Mex Restaurant in Texas: www.coastmonthly.com/2017/08/its-all-bueno; www.galvestonhistory.org/news/national-hispanic-american-heritage-month.

Oldest Butcher: abc13.com/abc13-plus-stantons-shopping-center-alvin-texas/5799235; www.alvinsun.net/news/article_e6c5d073-64e5-5329-aa46-1c2bb96675db.html; www.stantonmeats.com; www.tshaonline.org/handbook/entries/stanton-george-elliott; www.legacy.com/us/obituaries/houstonchronicle/name/flora-stanton-obituary?pid=292440.

Index

Airline Seafood, 68
Allen's Landing, 4–5, 149
Alley Theatre, 20, 25–26, 140
Antonio's Flying Pizza, 129
Astrodome, 82–84
Baker Botts, 12–13
Bayou Bend Collection and Gardens, 64–65
Brazos Bookstore, 89–90
Briar Shoppe, The, 81
Buffalo Bayou Park Cistern, 9, 40, 62–63
China Garden, 28–29
Christ Church Cathedral, 6–7
Christie's Seafood & Steaks, 123–124
Cleburne Cafeteria, 74–75
Church of the Annunciation, 14, 17
Congregation Beth Israel, 113–114
Daily News, The, 151–152
Diana Foundation, The, 79–80
Dolphin Fountain at Lamar Park, 76
Emancipation Park, 99, 100–101
Founders Memorial Cemetery, 35–36, 42
Freedmen's Town, 36–38, 42, 51
Gaido's Seafood Restaurant, 85, 165–166
Gilbert and Sullivan Society of Houston, 139–140
Glenwood Cemetery, 39–40, 42, 43–44
Griff's Irish Pub, 84
Gulf Freeway, 135–136
Gus Wortham Park Golf Course, 102–103, 121
Hamilton Shirts, 115–116
Harrisburg, TX, 149–150
Houston Art Car Parade, 32–33
Houston Buddhist Vihara, 145–146

Houston Country Club, 102, 120–122
Houston Fire Station No. 7, 49
Houston Grand Opera, 27
Houston Heights, 47–48, 135
Houston Symphony, 19–20, 57, 140
Houston This Is It Soul Food, 106–107
Humble Oil Field, 159–160
Imperial Sugar Co., 153–154
Incarnate Word Academy, 16–18
ISKCON of Houston, 87–88
James Coney Island, 54
J. Levy & Termini Funeral Home, 155–156
Kellum-Noble House, 8–9
Kennedy Bakery, 10–11
Kinkaid School, 40, 119–120
KUHT, 141–142
Leon's Lounge, 11, 77
Lynchburg Ferry, 148
Maida's, 45–46
Mai's Restaurant, 95
Masjid Warithuddeen Mohammed, 137–138
Miller Outdoor Theatre, 56–57
Moeller's Bakery, 69
Molina's Cantina, 127–128
Museum of Fine Arts, Houston, 58–59, 64
Niels Esperson Building, 23
Nielsen's Delicatessen, 78–94
Old Hanging Oak, 2–3
Old Sixth Ward, 40, 43–44, 50–51
Olivewood Cemetery, 41–42, 101
Original Kolache Shoppe, The, 134, 143–144

Original Mexican Cafe, The, 169
"Original" MLK Day Parade, 30–31
Original Ninfa's on Navigation, The, 108–109, 128
Pizzitola's Bar-B-Cue, 70
Prince's Hamburgers, 125–126
Ragin' Cajun, 93–94
Raja Sweets, 130–131
Rice University, 12, 52–53, 58, 110, 121
Rosenberg Library, 161–162
Sabine Street, 40, 50, 62
Saint Arnold Brewing Company, 33, 110–111
Sam Houston, The (hotel), 21–22
Sam Houston Monument, 60–61

Shepard's Barber Shop, 167–168
Shipley Do-Nuts, 73
Shudde Bros. Hatters, 163–164
Southland Hardware, 72
Stanton Meats, 170–171
Star Drug Store, 157–158
St. Joseph Medical Center, 18
SugarHill Recording Studios, 104–105
Third Planet Sci-Fi Superstore, 91–92
Tony's Restaurant, 85–86
Trinity United Methodist Church, 41, 98–99
West Alabama Ice House, 66–67
William P. Hobby Airport, 133–134
Woman's Club of Houston, The, 117–118